Rule of Law:

Navigating the Path to Justice

Rule of Law: Navigating the Path to Justice

Authors:

Bilal Ahmed

David Supina

Destiny Lenhardt

Erwin Kwok

Insiya Fathima Moosavi

Massa Mohamed Ali

Meera Chawda

Oana Padurean

Peter Anto Johnson

Rameen Tanveer

Yasir Omar

With

Austin Mardon & Catherine Mardon

PRESS

Typeset and cover design by Clare Dalton

Print ISBN: 978-1-77889-055-0

eBook ISBN: 978-1-77889-056-7

Golden Meteorite Press

103 11919 82 St NW

Edmonton, AB T5B 2W3

www.goldenmeteoritepress.com

Contents

Foreword

The common law is based on precedent caselaw developed over centuries, stemming back far into British medieval history. As the British Empire grew, so did the proliferation of "common" law. While significantly different from the past, the law remains the same in key aspects. One such similarity is the Rule of Law. This book introduces the significance of the Rule of Law, and what it is, and then delves into discussions from its early development until modernity. Important cases that have developed this principle, adhered to it, or even challenged it is also discussed. While by no means exhaustive, this book is intended to provide an overview to general audiences unfamiliar with the state of Western laws derived from the British Commonwealth; a system of laws based on the Rule of Law that is still in practice today. Join us as we guide readers on a historical journey through time in learning common law's growth.

Chapter 1: Preserving Justice- Introduction to the Rule of Law -

Yasir Omar

This chapter of the book went over a brief overview of the rule of law, its principles, significance, its application in the modern era and also its history of development across various civilizations and periods. It also discussed the role of rule of law and how it can enhance the quality of life of individuals and societies.

Overview

The rule of law is a fundamental principle of the philosophy of politics in which the law must be practised, carried out and respected by all layers of a society which includes the citizens, lawmakers, and heads of state who have a significant role in maintaining social order, creating and maintaining justice/equality/fairness, as well as protecting human rights. It is considered to be a crucial aspect of democracy in that it builds the basics of the legal and judicial system and most importantly how all residents live in harmony together in a community. Throughout this chapter, there will be a deeper introduction and analysis of this topic as well as some other topics related to this issue to help us to understand how it is implemented in modern societies.[1]

---

1   Tom Bingham, "The Rule of Law" (n.d.) online: *Google Books* <https://books.google.ca/books?hl=en&lr=&id=6UsjcX-IU-J4C&oi=fnd&pg=PT7&dq=what%2Bis%2Brule%2Bof%2Blaw&ots=736jo1Q-3e&sig=n549gU9bm9TE5agYcuf6JQ-0_Og&redir_esc=y#v=onepage&q=what%20is%20rule%20of%20law&f=false>.

The fundamental principles of the rule of law

As discussed earlier, the importance of the rule of law, mainly the rule of law is based upon some fundamentals which include and are not limited to transparency and accountability, equality before the law, legal certainty, conserving human rights, an independent judiciary, and separation of powers. Citizens and government officials need to work together, understand in theory and practice, feel responsible and practice the rule of law to make sure all these principles ensure that the basic principle of rule of law, which is establishing and conserving a just and equitable society. These principles include transparency and accountability, equality, certainty, human rights, impartiality, and division of powers.[2]

Transparency and accountability [3]

This principle refers to being truthful and honest in sharing government plans, decisions, or measures with the public in that everyone feels included and aware of what is happening. This can be hard and sometimes very challenging, but its benefits outweigh the cons and create stronger and united support for different communities. Government actions, plans, and rulings must be provided, accessible, and understandable to the public. This principle creates more responsibility, accountability and honesty across various government sections in which they all answer people which drastically lowers the chances for corruption and proves that all the lawmakers and government officials are working for the best interest of the nation and country.

---

2   Robert S Summers, "Principles of the rule of law" (n.d.) online: *Notre Dame Law Review* <https://scholarship.law.nd.edu/ndlr/vol74/iss5/11/>; Rojina Shrestha, "Rule of law: Definition, principles, characteristics, importance, advantages, challenges" (9 April 2022) online: *Public Health Notes* <https://www.publichealthnotes.com/rule-of-law-definition-principles-characteristics-importance-advantages-challenges/>.; Jeremy Waldron, "The rule of law" (22 June 2016) online: *Stanford Encyclopedia of Philosophy* <https://plato.stanford.edu/entries/rule-of-law/>.

3   *Ibid.*

There are important aspects of transparency and accountability in the framework of the law. One aspect is to encourage participation and engagement. This makes citizens feel more comfortable and inspired to participate in the decision-making process; elections and other forms of democratic processes as well as holding government officials accountable for their actions. Another aspect is to promote trust and legitimacy. When the government's actions and decisions are transparent, people will have faith and assurances in their government which further supports the legitimacy of the government in which the public servant would be held accountable. Preventing corruption is also important, as restrictions and preventative measures on government officials reduce the likelihood of them engaging in corrupt practices. Open, public discretion means violators are held accountable and face legal action and consequences. Finally, there is also the improvement of policy outcomes. This is making sure the government's actions and decisions are based on public input, accurate information, and sufficient evidence that serves the overall public interest.

Equality before the law [4]

Equality and impartiality of government provide equal opportunity and fairness across various layers of society regardless of race, colour, wealth, power, social status, or religious and political standings. All citizens are treated equally and are equal before the law, and no one is discriminated against. This principle guarantees that everyone receives and is subject to the same legal standards or services. This principle is important to prevent irresponsible and unnecessary use of power by lawmakers and government officials and provide protection and treatment under the law whenever necessary. There are various governmental and nongovernmental organizations working with the international community and even across the country to make sure the government and law are acting impartially and providing legal rights and protections for all citizens uniformly. Some various cases and

4   *Ibid.*

examples can be a good indicator that law is practised fairly, such
as the "right to a fair trial "(without considering their background
or circumstances), "equal protection of the law" (having the same
legal protections), and "non-discrimination", meaning that legislation or legal procedures should not segregate against individuals for their race, gender, religion, ethnicity, or any
other characteristic.

Legal certainty [5]

The law should be clear, unsurprising, and available to all people,
empowering them to figure out their privileges and commitments
and creating a trust bond between the government and the people.
It guarantees that people can comprehend their rights, privileges
and commitments and that they can design their activities appropriately. Likewise, it also expects that the law is applied reliably
and that people can anticipate similar lawful results in compa-
rable circumstances. This is important for keeping stability, and
social order, causing growth in the economy, and guaranteeing
that the general set of laws is available fairly and is reasonable
for everybody. One of the main requirements of legal certainly
revolves around the fact that all the laws and legislations subject
to citizens and organizations, should be clear and easily compre-
hendible by using coherent legal language and giving a simple
explanation of the complex legal terms and phrases. The legal
actions or consequences for every action should be predictable
and clear for people to avoid them. Legitimate certainty can be
favoured or advocated furthermore when the judicial system is
transparent and independent in all cases when the laws are practised or applied.

---

5   *Ibid.*

Conserving human rights [6]

Conserving and protecting human rights is the basis of rule of law that comprises political, civil, and economic rights. It ensures that individuals are protected from discrimination and the erratic or misuse of power by the government or other individuals. To ensure that justice is promoted and is not only in theory, there must be particular measures by the governments to enable organizations to work independently with no outside influence, to make sure the dignity of all residents is also conserved, and social order is maintained, human rights insured by the law must be respected. The correlation of human rights with the rule of law can be represented because of the interdependency of various human rights where the protection of one human right depends on the protection of other rights. The universalism of human rights is also relevant since human rights apply to people from different, cultures, religions, ethnicities and beliefs. This relates to the applicability and inalienability of human rights. These are guaranteed by the legal and judiciary systems in all situations, and when they are breached or violated by governments, individuals and organisations have the right to seek amendments.

Impartial judiciary system [7]

This is a system in which all the decision-making is fully based on facts and factual evidence and is not affected by political parties or threats. would increase people's trust in that they will be treated in a transparent process (all the process is done openly and is accessible to the public) that isn't affected by any external regulations or factors which avoids any biases and makes decisions fairly. Not being affiliated with any government or non-government organizations is important to establish a sense of equity, rationality (of working their cases regardless of their legal status in the country, accountability (not affected by threats or personal preferences or personal gains), background or history as well as any discriminatory reasons) and legitimacy across a country and

6   *Ibid.*
7   *Ibid.*

to further nurture the rule of law. To further increase the legitimacy and transparency of the judiciary system, some points that can be considered are the acquisition or recruitment of judicial officials based solely on merit and talent, adequate training accessible to officials that have an adequate understanding of principles or ethics, and most importantly a sense of security or tenure for the judges and their families to remove any sources that can influence the process and be able to serve the people and government they are answerable to.

Distribution of government powers [8]

To avoid dominancy and loss of control, establish balance to avoid any predominance of influence and power and ensure all branches use their powers within their jurisdiction and limits. There is also a need to divide responsibilities and power in a balanced manner; this is a way to prevent the abuse of rights and reduce the likelihood of authoritarianism. The efficiency of work these departments produce would be increased because they solely focus on particular sectors and government operations or tasks. It would also enable various branches of government to work closely together without interfering with each other's tasks and jurisdictions. This is a division of powers into three branches: legislative, executive, and judiciary. This principle ensures that no single branch of government has too much power and that there are checks and balances in place to prevent the abuse of power. The separation of powers is crucial for protecting individual rights, promoting democracy, and ensuring that government officials are held accountable for their actions. Establishing this feature can be done by creating constitutional limitations. Specifically, to clearly state each branch's responsibilities and limits of power. Supervision is conducted over these branches through the legislative and judicial wings of government, with clear and consistent checkups to remove and resolve any barriers toward the equal distribution of power and accountability of government branches.

---

8   *Ibid.*

The significance of the rule of law

As discussed earlier in this chapter, the rule of law is crucial for maintaining the fundamental components of the political and legal systems of a country (prosperity, stability, and democracy. There are multiple significances of the rule of law including accountability and prevention of abuse of government power; socio-political, and economic development to improve the overall standard of living of individuals; protection of human rights; empowerment of democracy and various freedoms to enable everyone to express their opinions and being able to hold the government accountable for their responsibilities, and; sustaining social order to provide residents with options for disputes and solve conflicts through legal means and holding people accountable with no exception or preferences for their actions, and punishing any illegal behaviour to promote social harmony and reduce conflicts.[9]

The relevance of the rule of law in modern societies

There is a strong correlation between rule of law and modern societies in which it ensures that the government is treating all the citizens fairly and importantly, the government is not abusing or mistreating their rights. This is done through a framework and a system of checks and balances (like the separation of powers inside the government). As emphasized earlier, this would play an important role both in the international and intranational status of a country by:

1. Strengthening stability and predictability across the nation: This would largely contribute toward the well-being of people. This can be done by holding people accountable for their actions and making it clear that there are measures against any illegal behaviour.[10]

---

9   Naomi Choi, "Rule of Law" (January 4, 2023) online: *Encyclopedia Britannica* <https://www.britannica.com/topic/rule-of-law>.

10   Abram Chayes, "The Modern Corporation and the Rule of

2. Establishing a healthy democracy: by providing various freedoms and making the government answerable to the nation and allowing individuals to participate in the democratic process.[11]

3. Creating opportunities for economic growth: through an increased level of investment from the private sector because the rule of law creates a stable and predictable legal environment for businesses and investors; this ensures contracts and property rights are protected. This also creates a large number of jobs across various industries which then leads to higher standards of living and decreased poverty levels in the country.[12]

4. Boosting accountability and transparency by working for the best interests of their country and people.[13]

5. Increasing respect for civil liberties: for instance, the freedom of speech or religion, protecting people against various discriminations like gender or ethnicity and protecting the dignity of individuals by preventing cases of arbitrary use of power and discrimination.[14]

6. Rule of law can also provide a platform for international communities to cooperate and debate regarding international trade, climate change, cybersecurity or common challenges/ topics. Additionally, it can

---

Law" (1 October 2013) online: *De Gruyter* <https://www.degruyter.com/document/doi/10.4159/harvard.9780674865204.c2/html>; Kishan Tiwari, "Article: Importance of Law in Society" (1 February 2017) online: *Legal Desire Media and Insights* <https://legaldesire.com/article-importance-of-law-in-society/>.

11   *Ibid.*

12   *Ibid.*

13   *Ibid.*

14   *Ibid.*

help to preserve peaceful co-existence and harmonic relationships between nations by providing resolutions of disputes between nations and making sure the laws are carried out and respected with the help of international courts.

History of the Development of the Rule of Law

Since the creation of the rule of law, there have been numerous times in which it was modified and restructured to make sure it meets the needs and demands of citizens across various time points in history. For example, in Babylon, the Code of Hammurabi created a system of justice that revolved around a set of rules and punishments proportional to the offence such as the principle of "an eye for an eye, a tooth for a tooth".[15] In ancient Egypt, a complex legal system was established by the pharaohs for running their society, they had punishments for anyone breaking the law and holding them accountable for their actions.[16] Likewise, the "Legalist school of thought" during the Warring States period in China, focused heavily on the significance of a legal system and written law when ruling a society.[17] In ancient times the rule

---

15　n.a., "Foundations of law and crime: Nature, elements and measurement" (2021) online: *Sage Publications* <https://uk.sagepub.com/sites/default/files/upmassets/110502_book_item_110502.pdf>; Joshua J Mark "Code of Hammurabi", (2019), online: *World History Encyclopedia* <https://www.worldhistory.org/Code_of_Hammurabi/>.

16　Ian Shaw, "The Oxford History of Ancient Egypt" (2003) online: *Google Books* <https://books.google.ca/books?hl=en&lr=&id=yugRDAAAQBAJ&oi=fnd&pg=P-P1&dq=Shaw%2C%2BI.%2B%282003%29.%2BThe%2BOx-ford%2BHistory%2Bof%2BAncient%2BEgypt.%2BOxford%2BUni-versity%2BPress.%2B&ots=UKy5aeHqX8&sig=d0N1exma0pnSo-jrJx7_sBQx9OHs#v=onepage&q=Shaw%2C%20I.%20(2003).%20The%20Oxford%20History%20of%20Ancient%20Egypt.%20Ox-ford%20University%20Press.&f=false>.

17　Yuri Pines, "Legalism in Chinese philosophy" (16 November 2018) online: *Stanford Encyclopedia of Philosophy* <https://plato.stanford.edu/entries/chinese-legalism/>.

of law can also be linked to ancient Greece and Roman civilizations, used primarily as a tool to ensure justice or fairness in society and prevent arbitrary rule.

These developments in the early stages established a foundation for the current modern political and legal systems. In Athens and Greece around 508 BCE, it was created by philosophers such as Cleisthenes, who believed that the law should be on the reason and applied equally to all citizens. He then presented a series of reforms such as the creation of the "Council of 500" that proposed and drafted laws to decrease the power of the traditional aristocracy and share it with common citizens.[18] The Roman Republic also constructed a legal system in which the principles were based on the "Twelve Tables", "*jus civile*" and "*ius gentium*". These laws were both for Romanian citizens and all individuals of various nationalities and social statuses that were all treated equally.[19]

---

18   Frowein, J. A., "The rule of law" (2003) *Max Planck Yearbook of United Nations Law*, 7(1), 1-34. <https://brill.com/view/journals/mpyo/19/1/article-pI_1.xml>; Mavroidis, P C (2017) Athenian democracy and the rule of law. In *Research Handbook on Law and Courts*, Edward Elgar Publishing at 29-48 <https://books.google.ca/books?hl=en&lr=&id=DoC4DwAAQBAJ&oi=fnd&pg=PR1&dq=Mavroidis,+P.+C.+(2017).+Athenian+democracy+and+the+rule+of+law.+In+Research+Handbook+on+Law+and+Courts+(pp.+29-48).+Edward+Elgar+Publishing.+&ots=UE9JeGZ2Q7&sig=kHuCJWs0mulb3pDiNFCb2lGKkek#v=onepage&q&f=false>.

19   Bernal M, "The History of the Rule of Law" (2019) online: *Oxford Research Encyclopedia* <https://oxfordre.com/politics/view/10.1093/acrefore/9780190228637.001.0001/acrefore-9780190228637-e-679>.; Tamanaha, Bian Z, "On the rule of law; History, Politics, Theory" (2004) online: *Google Books* <https://books.google.ca/books?hl=en&lr=&id=p4CReF-67hzQC&oi=fnd&pg=PA1&dq=History%2Bof%2Bthe%2Bdevelopment%2Bof%2Bthe%2Brule%2Bof%2Blaw%2B%2B&ots=B-bR6RP4z5M&sig=QRQuLpH8ZvZeXp7V0oH82jZzeKo#v=onepage&q=History%20of%20the%20development%20of%20the%20rule%20of%20law&f=fals>.

The development of the rule of law in Medieval Europe

There are various opinions and reports on the development of rule of law in medieval Europe in which some believe that Christian churches while others believe the creation of the common law system played an important role in its development which was beneficial for medical commerce, domestic or international trade to help solve any conflicts, just dealing, and implementation of the contracts through *"lex mercatoria"*, or the law merchant. Starting with the role of the Christian Church, was mainly through their immense influence on people that emphasized the point that all human beings were subject to the divine law or principles, and teachings of the Bible and Church and were mostly focused on working issues related to property, marriage, and ecclesiastical discipline through church's "Canon law" system, written laws and legal codes (such as *"Magna Carta"* in England written in 1215 for just treatment of everyone and limiting the monarchy power).[20]

It involved using, courts, legal institutions (Inquisition and ecclesiastical courts), judges, clergy and other members of the church to ensure the law is practised impartially. Moreover, there was a significant contribution from the common law system (the idea of previous legal decisions used to steer future decisions) in medieval Europe. Although the common law system was developed earlier in England, it quickly spread in Europe and around the world where the legal system became more complicated and needed a steadier and more predictable system. It was not based on specific laws or the arbitrary decisions of judges or rulers; it was based on the preceding judicial decisions of judges (authoritative sources of law), the practical experiences of lawyers and judges, legal reasoning and argumentation, which helped to

---

20   Bernal, M, "The History of the Rule of Law" (2019) online: *Oxford Research Encyclopedia* <https://oxfordre.com/politics/view/10.1093/acrefore/9780190228637.001.0001/acrefore-9780190228637-e-679>.; Tierney, B (2017) "The idea of natural rights: studies on natural rights, natural law, and church law" *Wm. B. Eerdmans Publishing* at 1150–1625 <https://journals.openedition.org/medievales/5818>.

promote the rule of law and the development of legal institutions and paved the path for the modern legal system.[21] To sum it all up, there were contributions from the church (which helped shape the legal values and standards), the common law system for legal practice, and even the secular legal systems.[22]

Development of the rule of law during the Enlightenment: 17th to early 19th century

Amidst numerous symbolic cultural and intellectual and cultural changes in Europe, the concept of belief in reason, individualism, progress, equality and justice gained more fame and so did the rule of law and written rules (legal positivism). There were various influencers and thinkers such as the French philosopher Montesquieu and John Locke, which advocated the avoidance of arbitrary rule, the subjectivity of the government to the law, the separation of powers across different branches of government, the protection of individual rights, ability to appeal and review the legal actions and decisions, natural rights (right to life, property, and liberty), consent of the governed, impartiality, and the sense of accountability of government toward its people.[23]

---

21   Zürn, M, A Nollkaemper & R Peerenboom, "Rule of Law Dynamics: In an Era of International and Transnational Governance" (2012) *Springer Press* at 13-30 <https://books.google.ca/books?hl=en&lr=&id=pAAgAwAAQBAJ&oi=fnd&pg=PR9&d-q=+In+an+Era+of+International+and+Transnational+Governance&ots=pEWgwQVqj3&sig=a5hGbPIfee1nQXpwi0KWE92T-k7g#v=onepage&q=In%20an%20Era%20of%20International%20and%20Transnational%20Governance&f=false>.; n.a., "Law and Religion: Law and Religion in Medieval Europe" (2023) online: *Encyclopedia.com* <https://www.encyclopedia.com/environment/ency-clopedias-almanacs-transcripts-and-maps/law-and-religion-law-and-re-ligion-medieval-europe>.

22   Carol Symes, "The rule of law in medieval England" (24 February 2023) online: *Wondrium Daily* <https://www.wondriumdaily.com/the-rule-of-law-in-medieval-england/>.

23   Matthew White, "The Enlightenment" (21 June 2018) online: *British Library* <https://www.bl.uk/restoration-18th-century-literature/

Development of the rule of law in the modern era: post-Enlightenment period

As the legal and political system became more and more complicated and sophisticated, the modern era, particularly after World War II, also provided opportunities for the development of the rule of the law such as the national constitution of the United States and France to defend and preserve human rights.[24] As the number of governmental and non-governmental organizations and establishments such as the United Nations, international human rights or other international treaties and declarations for enshrining justice, security, and development increased, many new laws and regulations such as international law was created in the global legal system that is crucial in boosting global cooperation and solving matters between nations diplomatically and harmoniously. The United Nations Rule of Law Assistance program and the *Universal Declaration of Human Rights* asserted that "everyone is entitled to a fair and public hearing by an independent and impartial tribunal, in the determination of his rights and obligations and of any criminal charge against him" were also established to empower legal systems in countries when needed.[25] Some key developments that helped shape the modern era's rule of law include international tribunals, international law, technology, separation of powers, and the availability of legal representation.[26]

International Tribunals like the International Court of Justice and the International Criminal Court have the capacity and power to

---

articles/the-enlightenment>.

24   Bruce Ackerman, "The rise of world constitutionalism" (1997) online: *JSTOR* <https://www.jstor.org/stable/1073748>; Massimo Tommasoli, "Rule of law and democracy: Addressing the gap between policies and practices" (December 2012) online: *United Nations* <https://www.un.org/en/chronicle/article/rule-law-and-democracy-addressing-gap-between-policies-and-practices>.

25   *Ibid.*

26   United Nations, "Universal Declaration of Human Rights" (n.d.) online: *United Nations* <https://www.un.org/en/about-us/universal-declaration-of-human-rights>.

hold people and states accountable for any transgressions of legal and human rights obligations.[27] International Law and Human Rights by the foundation of the United Nations emphasized the importance of human rights in rule of law and international law. Progress in technology as well has played a significant role in the progression of the rule of law by providing means of accessing and sharing legal information and providing links to communication among legal professionals. This also causes some concerns about privacy and cybercrime. Finally, there is a separation of powers arising from the ideas of Montesquieu that have helped avoid abuses of power through Constitutional development.[28] This relates to the availability of legal representation. Creating more ways for access to justice has enhanced the rule of law in social justice and economic development. The help of legal aid programs enables individuals from lower economical classes to have legal representation in much the same way as individuals from other classes.

---

27   *Ibid.*

28   *Ibid.*

Chapter 2: Defining the Rule of Law

Oana Padurean

The Elements of the Rule of Law

The concept of "rule of law" has many contested definitions. However, in its simplest and most basic form, it means maintaining a just society where citizens or government officials cannot be considered to be above the law. Every man, regardless of rank or condition, is subject to the ordinary law of the land and must comply with the jurisdiction of the ordinary tribunals. Based on this premise, all civilians are subject to the same law administered in the same courts. This explanation is believed to be the general premise that makes up the concept of the "rule of law."

By definition, the "rule of law" implies that a system of laws is in place. This, by nature, involves a set of rules that are determined in advance and are stated in general terms. Important to acknowledge is that the law must be generally known and understood. The requirements imposed by the law cannot be impossible for people to meet and follow. In addition, the laws must be applied equally to every one according to the terms. Lastly, there must be mechanisms and institutions in place that enforce the legal rules in place when they are breached. All of these factors make up a simplified understanding of what is known as the "rule of law." However, this notion can be further broken down into more specific categories.

1. The supremacy of the law and its application to all

The rule of law is an umbrella term used for many legal and institutional instruments to protect citizens against the power of the state. Commonly, the rule of law is embraced within liberalism and capitalist societies.[29] Its purpose is to protect citizens' property and lives from infringements and assaults by fellow citizens and government officials alike. In these liberalist societies, each individual is advised on the permissible range of free action. Without a pre-existing law that specifies whether or not a particular action is prohibited, there can be no criminal punishment. Accordingly, every citizen is free to do whatever they would like insofar as the stated rules are not violated.

To portray this idea alternately, a contrast can be drawn between the "rule of law" and the "rule of man".[30] This opposition refers to the notion that to live under the rule of law is to not be subjected to the unpredictable whims of other individuals – this includes monarchs, judges, government officials, or fellow citizens. This concept shields an individual from biases, passions, prejudice, error, or ignorance. With the power to rule over others comes the potential for its abuse and the rise of corruption. The idea of the "rule of law, not man" accepts that human participation in the process is inevitable.[31] However, to avoid flawed and corrupted self-interpretation, power is divided into various branches that undergo a series of checks and balances.

---

29   [1] Lord Bingham, "The rule of law" (2007) 66:1 *The Cambridge Law Journal* at 78 [*Bingham*].

30   Richard H. Fallon, "'The rule of law' as a concept in constitutional discourse" (1997) 97:1 *Columbia Law Review* at 3 [*Fallon*].

31   Brian Z. Tamanaha, "The history and elements of the rule of law" (2012) *SSRN Electronic Journal* at 233 [*Tamanaha*].

2.   *The equality of all before the law*

To restrain government tyranny, the rule of law operates under the notion of equality of all. This in turn limits the sovereign, the state, and its officials to follow the laws in place. Restraining the sovereign's power has been a perennial struggle for societies for as long as they have existed.[32] Accordingly, the efforts to impose legal limits on the sovereign expose an ancient dilemma: the sovereign creates the law, so how can the creator of the law be bound by the law? Two distinct features have been identified to explain this question. Firstly, the sovereign and government officials must operate within a limiting framework of the law. The law can change when done by authorized officials following appropriate procedures, but it must be complied with until the change(s) is enacted. Secondly, if there is a desire to change the laws, government officials are not entirely free to change them in any way they desire. There are specified restraints on their law-making power. In contemporary society, these restraints are defined by human rights, constitutional rights or limitations.[33] The fundamental takeaway from this feature is that the sovereign's power subjects itself to higher legal restrictions.

Furthermore, the contemporary world has also found different solutions to hold the sovereign to the law. This solution involves the creation of distinct institutions within the government with specific law-related functions. This institutionalization differentiates the sovereign and the government itself, thereby obliging each party to enforce the law. In many societies today, this involves the office of the Attorney General or the prosecutor, which may be under the authority of the Executive.[34] In addition to an independent prosecuting branch within the government, an independent judicial branch exists in many societies. Within this branch, judges have the duty to apply the law.

---

32   *Ibid* at 236.

33   *Ibid* at 237.

34   *Bingham, supra* note 1 at 67.

3. *The independence and impartiality of the judiciary*

It is necessary to understand that there is an essential prerequisite that the judiciary must possess, this being a degree of independence from the rest of the governmental apparatus. Having this structural partitioning from the government implies that the judiciary can hold accountable the other parts on legal grounds. Essentially, the judge becomes the law personified.[35] After extensive training in legal knowledge and the craft of judging, a judge takes the oath to decide cases according to the law.

To make these legal decisions, the judiciary can have no discretion for the facts on which a decision-maker, official, or judicial proceeds. Of course, it may be necessary to have an assessment of the facts, but this would depend on the effect of the evidence being presented and how it is perceived by the decision-maker. The assessment may or may not be correct, however, if the evidence leads the decision-maker to one conclusion then they have no discretion to reach another. Furthermore, these discretions depend on the making of a prior judgement. Once made, the course of action is set into motion which leaves no room for choice.

The Rule of Law and International Law

1. *The relationship between domestic and international law*

The relationship between domestic and international law is complex and necessary to differentiate. A preliminary distinction between the two recognizes that the rule of law within national legal systems has been fully developed whereas international rule of law continues to be in the making.[36] Such is the case because the rule of law functions to protect the rights of individuals who would otherwise go against an all-powerful governing authority.[37]

35   *Tamanaha, supra* note 3 at 244.

36   Arthur Watts, "The International Rule of Law" (1993) 36 *German YB Int'l L* at 16 [*Watts*].

37   James Crawford, Judith Gardam, and Hilary Charlesworth,

Additionally, more specific legislations which have been determined as part of the rule of law often reflect a state's historical and constitutional evolution.[38] As a result, the rule of law would differ from state to state. There is no one national meaning of the concept, therefore it is impossible to perfectly apply it at an international level. With that said, the understanding of international rule of law has evolved and has become more intertwined with the domestic understanding of rule of law.

Originally, international law was perceived to consist of laying down the boundary conditions for state conflict and coexistence. These boundaries consisted of the establishment of laws of war, peace treaties, territorial boundaries, immunities of representation, etc.[39] Nevertheless, this understanding has developed over time. International law has increasingly become more concerned with matters internal to the state – including human rights, the environment, investment protection, criminal law, intellectual property, and others.[40] In many of these fields, the role of international law is in fact to reinforce, and at times institute, the rule of law domestically. This brings about the question: Should international law embody the standards set for national systems? Or, is it possible for international law to accept that the rule of law is a virtue of national systems which international law can enforce without having to comply with it?

One instance where this question was answered was in the International Criminal Tribunal for the Former Yugoslavia (ICTY). The issue presented was whether the ICTY was 'established by law' within the meaning of Article 14 of the *International Covenant on Civil and Political Rights* (ICCPR).[41] After adjudicating the case, the ICTY found that international human rights standards are set for national, not international courts. It said:

"International law and the rule of law" (2003) 24:1 *Adelaide Law Review* at 7 [*Crawford, Gardam, and Charlesworth*].

38   Simon Chesterman, "An International Rule of Law?" (2008) 56:2 *American journal of comparative law* at 358 [*Chesterman*].

39   *Crawford, Gardam, and Charlesworth, supra* note 8 at 7.

40   *Ibid* at 7.

41   *Ibid* at 9.

"[T]he principle that a tribunal must be established by law [...] is a general

principle of the law imposing an international obligation which only applies to the administration of criminal justice in a municipal setting".[42]

While this statement was made, it cannot be wholly accepted that international institutions, including judicial institutions, are exempt from international standards. This brings up the question of how international organizations interact with the rule of law and promote it.

2.   *The role of international organizations in promoting the rule of law*

When the rule of law extends to the international forum, international organizations participate to promote numerous different functions. They exist to solidify the foundation for a rights-respected state, enable economic growth, and serve as a form of conflict resolution.[43] These categories are to be further examined to contextualize the role of international organizations in promoting the rule of law.

A. Creating a rights-respected state by upholding human rights

The rule of law can be more broadly identified as a set of ideals, understood in terms of protecting human rights. The 1948 *Universal Declaration of Human Rights* specifies human rights to consist of the prohibition of arbitrary deprivation of liberty,

42   *Ibid* at 9.
43   *Chesterman, supra* note 9 at 343.

requiring fair trials by independent and impartial tribunals, and protecting equality before the law.[44] The 1948 Universal Declaration is consistent with most subsequent general human rights treaties, legitimizing it as an international document that supports the rule of law. Comparingly, in the eyes of the United Nations, the rule of law in correspondence to human rights is defined as:

> "…a principle of governance in which all persons, institutions and entities, public and private, including the State itself, are accountable to laws that are publicly promulgated, equally enforced and independently adjudicated, and which are consistent with international human rights norms and standards."[45]

These two definitions lend themselves to understanding how human rights fit into promoting international rule of law, and how international organizations participate in this process. For instance, in the 1993 Vienna World Conference on Human Rights, the United Nations had been recommended to offer technical and financial assistance upon request to national projects. These projects would seek to "reform penal and correctional establishments, educate and train lawyers, judges and security forces on human rights" and assist any other sphere directly relevant to the rule of law.[46] In this manner, the connection between the national and international was routinized as it set the precedent for the General Assembly to enforce these values internationally through domestic initiatives.

---

44   *Ibid* at 343.

45   *Tamanaha, supra* note 3 at 234.

46   *Chesterman, supra* note 9 at 60.

B. Economic growth

The rule of law has long been seen as the vehicle for promoting economic growth. This is because the idea of formal legality in collaboration with the right to property and independent judiciary leads to economic development.[47] However, there is a struggle to come up with objective criteria to measure the rule of law in the context of economics. The 1992 Human Development Report established by the U.N. Development Program underlined five possible indicators to help define it: (1) fair and public hearings in criminal cases, (2) a competent, independent, and impartial judiciary, (3) the availability of legal counsel, (4) provisions for review of convictions in criminal cases, and (5) if government officials are prosecuted when they violate the rights and freedoms of other peoples.[48] As per the report, fulfilling these criteria upholds people's dignity while also enabling them to fulfil their legitimate aspirations.[49]

Since 1997, the development community began using the term "good governance" when referring to a set of activities that embrace participation, transparency, and accountability in government.[50] The term "good governance" has emerged with the development discourse as a means of expanding the prescription of donors to embrace not just projects but government policies. In this way, having a modern state formal legality can introduce the certainty required for economic development.[51] Accordingly, intergovernmental organizations such as the World Bank and the International Monetary Fund must then act in correspondence to the criteria laid out to promote good governance in political processes. Having good governance and the rule of law at the national and international level is then inferred to be a necessity for sustained economic growth and the eradication of poverty.

---

47   Adriaan Bedner, "An elementary approach to the rule of law" (2010) 2:1 *Hague Journal on the Rule of Law* at 60 [*Bedner*].

48   *Chesterman, supra* note 9 at 347.

49   *Ibid.*

50   *Ibid* at 347.

51   *Bedner, supra* note 18 at 60.

C. Conflict Resolution

The rule of law encompasses the national and international when it comes to sustaining peace and security. In the same vein that a state would want to increase its prosperity and safeguard its security, the preservation of international peace and security should not be viewed as an altruistic desire.[52] Rather, it should be seen as the interest of the state considering that conditions of stability can only be established collectively. To achieve this collective cohesion, Article 2(7) of the U.N. Charter states that it excludes matters specifically under domestic jurisdiction, but U.N. interference is acceptable to maintain international peace and security under Chapter VII.[53] Since the mid-1990s, the coercive powers that the Security Council holds have been used to support, supplant, or replace domestic legal systems to align with the international agenda. The first instance where the Security Council used the words "rule of law" were in the operative paragraph of resolution 1040 where it expressed its support for the Security General's efforts to have national reconciliation, democracy, security, and the rule of law in Burundi.[54] Subsequently, many peace operations in states like Guatemala, Liberia, and Côte D'Ivoire have called for the re-establishment or the restoration and maintenance of the rule of law. In these circumstances, it is important to note that for the international rule of law to be invoked by organizations, states must consent to the authority being exercised over them.[55] This may be in the form of accepting interference through peace operations, or if member states are recognized to be a part of the United Nations.

1. The challenges of enforcing international law

As previously discussed, the rule of law certainly is present in national legal systems, but is rather weak in terms of international

---

52   *Watts, supra* note 8 at 24.

53   *Chesterman, supra* note 9 at 348.

54   *Ibid* at 348.

55   *Watts, supra* note 8 at 32.

law. This is because international treaty laws are what bind states to fulfil certain obligations. However, the use of a treaty form does not itself ensure hard obligation.[56] If a treaty is to be regarded as "hard," it must be precisely worded and specify the exact obligations that the state must carry out or the rights that are being granted. The problem at hand is that the Vienna Convention on the Law of Treaties does not require that the treaties between states establish narrowly defined rights and obligations.[57] As a result, the use of treaties only provides the formation of gradual standards and the expectation for general goals. Legal enforcement becomes a difficult task to achieve when the rule of law relies on international treaty laws. On one hand, legal enforcement can happen at the domestic level and domestic actors may choose to use their country's legal system to enforce the terms of international law agreements.[58] Alternatively, international bodies and states who are party to the treaty may respond to the violations in the ways that are described in the treaty, but this decision is based primarily on the state's executive choice.[59] The overall process of treaties is unreliable given that countries may fail to join treaties to which they could easily comply (because of little gains and greater losses), or they may join treaties that they have little inclination to obey (having too much to gain and little to lose).[60]

When making comparisons, this commitment does not operate in the same manner as customary international law. The most apparent reason is that this type of law is a general practice accepted by all, which has become a norm over time. To achieve this, there must be sufficient evidence of state practice and *opinion juris*.[61] State practice consists of evidence of what states do and what they say. When there is enough evidence to suggest a consistent and uniform body of state practice, and *opinion juris* establishes a

56   Christine M Chinkin, "The challenge of Soft Law: Development and change in international law" (1989) 38:4 *International and Comparative Law Quarterly* at 851 [*Chinkin*].

57   *Ibid* at 851.

58   Oona A Hathaway, "Between power and principle" (2011) *The Role of Ethics in International Law* at 473 [*Hathaway*].

59   *Ibid* at 473.

60   *Ibid* at 474.

61   *Chinkin, supra* note 27 at 857.

subjective obligation, then the state is bound to the law in question. Of course, states may avoid the application of customary international law by persistently objecting to following it. This is known as the persistent objector rule which is "an accepted application of the traditional principle that international law essentially depends on the consent of the states".[62] However, this puts the state at great risk of being rejected by the international collective body. For this reason, this threat is sufficient to ensure that states follow customary international law.

---

62   *Hathaway, supra* note 29 at 348.

Chapter 3: The Role of the Judiciary

Destiny Lenhardt

Introduction

The judiciary comprises federal and provincial courts and operates independently from the legislative and executive branches of government. The judiciary is a critical branch of government tasked with interpreting and applying laws to resolve disputes between parties. The judiciary must uphold the rule of law, protect individual rights, and ensure the proper functioning of government institutions.[63] This chapter of the book delves into the significance of maintaining the independence of the judiciary, the judiciary's responsibility in safeguarding the rule of law, and examples that demonstrate these principles in practice.

Importance of Judicial Independence

As discussed in the earlier chapter, judicial independence is essential for ensuring the proper functioning of the judiciary and upholding the rule of law. Judicial independence means that judges are free from political influence or interference and can make decisions based solely on the law and the facts of the case. This

---

63   Canadian Judicial Council, "Ethical Principles for Judges" (2004) online: *Canadian Judicial Council* <https://cjc-ccm.ca/cmslib/general/news_pub_judicialconduct_Principles_en.pdf>.

independence is necessary to ensure that the judiciary remains impartial and fair and is not subject to external pressures that could compromise its integrity.

The Role of Judges in Upholding the Rule of Law

Judges are responsible for interpreting and applying laws fairly and impartially. Their decisions can have a profound impact on individuals and society as a whole. Judges are essential for the proper functioning of the legal system and the administration of justice. The judicial selection process is designed to ensure that only individuals with exceptional qualifications and a high level of integrity are appointed as judges. Consequently, the qualifications and procedures involved in becoming a judge are thorough and demand significant time and diligence. This involves extensive education, legal experience, and a rigorous vetting process that includes evaluations of the candidate's legal knowledge, ethical conduct, and character.

To ensure judges hold this exceptional level of knowledge, the Canadian Judicial Council outlines the vitality of judicial diligence involving the proactive steps in enhancing the education and knowledge of judges, as well as improving the expertise, abilities, and mindset necessary for effective legal adjudication.[64] This entails engaging in ongoing educational initiatives and private study. Further, the Canadian Judicial Council delineates the criteria by which judges are expected to adhere to when ensuring the enforcement of the rule of law through just and unbiased application of laws.[65] In Canada, only after practising as a lawyer and maintaining good standing with The Federation of Law Societies of Canada will the federal government consider appointing a judge to the federal courts, the superior courts of the provinces/ territories, or the Supreme Court of Canada.[66]

64   *Ibid.*

65   *Ibid.*

66   Government of Canada, Department of Justice, "Canada's Court System" (2021) online: *Government of Canada* <https://www. justice.gc.ca/eng/csj-sjc/ccs-ajc/index.html>.

According to the Canadian Judicial Council (CJC), a fundamental objective of judges is to analyze and interpret intricate legal issues and apply legal principles in a consistent and unbiased manner.[67] Judges must remain impartial and not succumb to political pressure or personal prejudices.[68] Their decisions must be solely based on the law and the facts presented in each case, while also ensuring that all parties have an opportunity to present their case and be heard in court. As interpreters of the law, judges possess the power to examine the language and meaning of statutes, regulations, and legal precedents, while also considering the intent and purpose of the law in their decision-making process. By ensuring that the law is applied equally and fairly to all individuals, regardless of their social status, race, or gender, judges play a critical role in upholding the rule of law. Through impartial and equitable decision-making, judges help to foster public trust in the legal system and promote societal stability and fairness. Additionally, judges are responsible for enforcing the law and holding accountable those who violate it, thus further upholding the rule of law.

How judges uphold the rule of law

Judges play a vital role in upholding the law and ensuring that those who violate it are held accountable. Gall outlines the range of means that judges use to uphold the law, including adjudicating cases, imposing sentences or remedies, interpreting the law, overseeing legal proceedings and applying the law in various cases.[69] In criminal, civil, and administrative cases, judges preside over trials and hearings. They are responsible for hearing evidence, determining the facts of the case, and applying the law to make decisions or render judgments. Additionally, judges have the authority to impose sentences on convicted individuals in

---

67   *Ibid.*

68   Gerald Gall, "Judiciary in Canada" (2006) online: *The Canadian Encyclopedia* <https://www.thecanadianencyclopedia.ca/en/article/judiciary>.

69   *Ibid.*

criminal cases and order remedies such as injunctions, damages, or specific performance in civil cases. Superior court judges are held accountable for their actions and decisions, as hearings, trials, and rulings are subject to public scrutiny. This allows for transparency and accountability, ensuring that justice is seen to be done, and providing an avenue for citizens and the media to discuss and critique the work of the courts. If a judge's ruling is deemed unsatisfactory, it can be appealed to a higher court. If an error has been made, a new trial will be ordered, or the decision will be corrected to ensure that justice is fairly and impartially administered.[70]

Breaking Judicial Independence

If a judge makes a biased decision, it could have serious conse-quences. It could lead to an appeal of the decision, which could result in a higher court overturning the decision. It could also lead to a loss of public trust in the judiciary, which is essential for maintaining the rule of law. A biased decision could also create a perception of unfairness and discrimination, which could harm the reputation of the court and the legal system as a whole. In ex-treme cases, it could even result in calls for the judge's impeach-ment or removal from the bench.[71]

Despite the extensive judicial selection process, there have been instances of judges not following judicial independence. In 2003, Judge Moore, who was then the Chief Justice of the Alabama Supreme Court, refused to comply with a federal court order to remove a Ten Commandments monument from the state court-house.[72] He believed that the monument represented the moral

70   "Canada's Justice System." *The Canadian Superior Courts Judges Association (CSCJA)*, https://cscja.ca/canadas-justice-system/.

71   Peter Green and John Mazor. "Corrupt Justice: What Happens When Judges' Bias Taints a Case?" *The Guardian*, Guardian News and Media, 18 Oct. 2015, https://www.theguardian.com/us-news/2015/oct/18/judge-bias-corrupts-court-cases.

72   Joan Biskupic, "Roy Moore: The Judge Who Fought the Law | CNN Politics." *CNN*, Cable News Network, 27 Sept. 2017, https://

foundation of the law and was therefore a protected expression of religious freedom. However, by refusing to comply with a federal court order, Judge Moore violated the principle of judicial independence, which requires judges to be impartial and to follow the law, even when they disagree with it. His actions brought criticism from legal scholars, judicial watchdog groups, and civil liberties advocates.

The implications of Judge Moore's actions were significant. He was removed from his position as Chief Justice of the Alabama Supreme Court and was disciplined by the Alabama Judicial Inquiry Commission. Most importantly, his defiance of the court order impacted taxpayers with a lengthy proceeding. It created a constitutional crisis and undermined the public's trust in the judiciary.[73]

Introduction to Canadian Jurisprudence

The word jurisprudence means "practical wisdom about law". Canadian Jurisprudence refers to the study and interpretation of the Canadian legal system focusing on topics such as the general characteristics of legal rules, norms, systems and institutions; and topics of legal reasoning, decision-making, validity, rights and interpretation. Jurisprudence has taken on heightened significance in Canada since the implementation of the Canadian *Charter of Rights and Freedoms*. The *Charter* has made the moral justification of legal norms and decisions a crucial component of Canadian law. While certain *Charter* rulings have generated controversy, the Canadian legal system as a whole has demonstrated an aptitude for utilizing jurisprudential principles to guide the practice of law.[74] Canada is a common law country that combines civil law. This means that its legal system is based on precedent and the decisions of judges in previous cases. The Canadian legal

---

www.cnn.com/2017/09/27/politics/roy-moore-judicial-fight/index.html.

73   *Ibid.*

74   Roger A Shiner, "Jurisprudence". *The Canadian Encyclopedia*, 16 December 2013, *Historica Canada*. www.thecanadianencyclopedia.ca/en/article/jurisprudence. Accessed 04 April 2023.

system is also influenced by the country's unique history, culture, and political system.[75]

Living Tree vs Original Intent Interpretation

One of the central debates in Canadian Jurisprudence is between the living tree and original intent interpretations of the Constitution. The living tree doctrine holds that the Constitution is a living document that evolves to reflect changing social, cultural, and political values. In this approach, the courts interpret the Constitution in light of its underlying principles and purposes, rather than its original meaning. The original intent doctrine, on the other hand, holds that the Constitution should be interpreted according to its original meaning, as understood by the framers at the time of its drafting. In this approach, the courts should interpret the Constitution based on its plain and ordinary meaning, without regard to contemporary values or social context. The debate between these two approaches has been a central theme in Canadian Jurisprudence for many years. While some judges and legal scholars argue that the living tree doctrine is necessary to ensure that the Constitution remains relevant in a changing world, others argue that the original intent doctrine is necessary to preserve the original meaning and intent of the Constitution.[76]

The Constitution and the Role of the Judiciary

According to the Government of Canada, the Constitution is the supreme law of Canada, and it sets out the framework for the country's legal and political system. The Constitution is upheld by the role of the judiciary in interpreting and applying the rule of law. The rule of law is a fundamental principle of Canadian

75   *Canada's System of Justice.* Department of Justice Canada, 2015, https://www.justice.gc.ca/eng/csj-sjc/just/img/courten.pdf.

76   Bradley W Miller, "Beguiled by Metaphors: The 'Living Tree' and Originalist Constitutional Interpretation in Canada." *Canadian Journal of Law and Jurisprudence*, vol. 22, no. 2, 2009, pp. 331–354., https://doi.org/10.1017/s0841820900004720.

Jurisprudence, which holds that everyone is subject to the law and that the law must be applied impartially and consistently. The Canadian Judicial Council outlines the role that the judiciary plays in upholding the rule of law by abiding by the Constitution and applying it to specific cases. The judiciary also has the power to strike down laws that violate the fundamental principles of the Constitution. This power is an important safeguard against government overreach and the violation of individual rights.

Judicial Decisions that Upheld the Rule of Law

Duignan discusses *Brown v. Board of Education*. This case was a landmark in United States history that overturned the legal doctrine of "separate but equal" and ended racial segregation in public schools.[77] The case was decided by the Supreme Court of the United States in 1954, and its ruling had far-reaching implications for civil rights and the rule of law in America. Starting in the late 1940s, the National Association for the Advancement of Colored People (NAACP) launched a focused initiative aimed at challenging segregated school systems in multiple states, including Kansas. A group of African American parents in Topeka, Kansas, filed a lawsuit on behalf of their children against the local Board of Education when their African-American children were denied acceptance into the White school. The parents argued that the Board's policy of segregating schools based on race violated the constitutional rights of their children. The case eventually made its way to the Supreme Court, along with three other class-action school-segregation lawsuits in 1952. In May 1954, the Court issued its unanimous decision, holding that segregation in public schools violated the Equal Protection Clause of the Fourteenth Amendment to the United States Constitution. The Court overturned its previous ruling in *Plessy v. Ferguson*, which had upheld the constitutionality of separate but equal facilities for different races.

---

77   Brian Duignan, "Brown v. Board of Education." *Encyclopædia Britannica*, Encyclopædia Britannica, Inc., 7 Mar. 2023, https://www. britannica.com/event/Brown-v-Board-of-Education-of-Topeka.

There were protests and backlash from the people afterwards the *Brown* decision but it was a critical moment in the history of the United States. It established the principle that segregation was inherently unequal and violated the constitutional rights of African Americans. The decision also established the Supreme Court's authority to interpret the Constitution and declare laws unconstitutional. The *Brown v. Board of Education* decision had a significant impact on civil rights and the rule of law in the United States. The *Brown* decision not only ended racial segregation in public schools but it helped promote diversity and inclusion in American society.[78] This decision helped break down barriers that had long divided communities and helped create more inclusive and integrated schools and communities. The *Brown* decision was a watershed moment in the struggle for civil rights, inspiring many subsequent legal challenges to discrimination and inequality.

The decision paved the way for a variety of social and political changes that continue to impact American society today. Further, the *Brown* decision established the principle that the Constitution guarantees equal protection under the law for all citizens, regardless of race or ethnicity. This principle has become a cornerstone of American law and is essential for maintaining the rule of law and promoting justice and fairness in society. The *Brown* decision was a crucial example of how judicial decisions can uphold the rule of law by protecting individual rights and liberties, even when such protections are controversial or unpopular. The decision also demonstrates the importance of judicial independence in safeguarding the Constitution and ensuring that the law is applied equally to all individuals.[79]

In summary, the *Brown v. Board of Education* decision remains an important legal precedent and a symbol of progress and change in American history.[80] The decision had a significant

---

78   *Ibid.*

79   William Kashatus, "The Long-Term Legacies of Brown v. Board." *Origins*, 2004, https://origins.osu.edu/history-news/long-term-legacies-brown-v-board?language_content_entity=en.

80   *Ibid.*

impact on civil rights, the rule of law, and social progress, and its legacy continues to influence American society today.

Landmark Case in Canada

There have been many landmark cases in Canadian Jurisprudence that upheld the rule of law and shaped the country's legal and political system. One such example is the *Reference re Persons* Case. In 1927, five women, known as the "Famous Five," asked the Canadian government to appoint them to the Senate. However, their request was denied as they were not "qualified persons" under Section 24 of the *British North America Act*. The women challenged this decision in court, arguing that the word "persons" in Section 24 should be interpreted to include women. In Edmonton, they signed a petition that was sent off to the governor-general. After denial, the appeal was sent to the Judicial Committee of the Privy Council, the highest authority. The committee decided that the word "persons" in Section 24 should indeed be interpreted to include women and that women were therefore eligible for appointment to the Senate. The *Persons* Case was a significant victory for women's rights in Canada, as it established that women were legally considered "persons" under the law and entitled to the same rights and privileges as men. The decision paved the way for women's increased participation in Canadian politics and public life.[81]

The case also had broader implications for Canadian constitutional law. It established that the Canadian Constitution was a living document that could be interpreted to reflect changing social and political values, rather than being strictly limited to its original meaning. This is an application to the living tree approach to constitutional interpretation which has been influential in shaping Canadian constitutional law ever since. The *Reference re Persons* case was a landmark decision by the Supreme Court of Canada in 1985, which held that the Canadian *Charter of Rights and Free-*

---

81   David Cruickshank and Tabitha de Bruin. "Persons Case." *The Canadian Encyclopedia*, 7 Feb. 2006, https://www.thecanadianencyclo-pedia.ca/en/article/persons-case.

doms protects the rights of all individuals, including those who are not Canadian citizens or permanent residents.[82] This decision was important because it recognized that the *Charter* is a fundamental part of the Canadian legal system and that it protects the rights of everyone subject to Canadian law.

Overturning of Landmark Judicial Decision

Encyclopedia Britannica discusses the evolution of *Roe v. Wade*; a landmark decision by the United States Supreme Court in 1973 that established a constitutional right to abortion.[83] The decision held that a state law banning abortion, except to save the life of the mother, was unconstitutional because it violated a woman's right to privacy, which the court found to be protected by the Due Process Clause of the Fourteenth Amendment. The *Roe v. Wade* decision was significant in that it upheld the rule of law by establishing that the Constitution protects certain fundamental rights, including the right to privacy, and that these rights are enforceable through the courts. The decision also affirmed the principle that women have the right to make decisions about their bodies without undue interference from the government. The benefits of the *Roe v. Wade* decision include increased access to safe and legal abortion services, which have been shown to reduce maternal mortality rates and improve women's health outcomes. The decision also helped to reduce the stigma associated with abortion and gave women greater control over their reproductive lives.

However, since *Roe v. Wade* was decided, there have been ongoing challenges to its legality and attempts to restrict access to abortion. As an illustration, the Court supported the constitutionality of the federal *Partial-Birth Abortion Ban Act* of 2003, which prohibited the utilization of a scarcely employed method of abor-

---

82   *Ibid.*

83   Encyclopedia Britannica, "*Roe v. Wade.*" *Encyclopedia Britannica*, Encyclopedia Britannica Inc., 26 Mar. 2023, https://www.britannica.com/biography/Norma-McCorvey.

tion called intact dilation and evacuation.[84] In more recent years, several states have passed laws that place significant restrictions on abortion, and there has been a concerted effort to overturn the decision by appointing conservative justices to the Supreme Court. In 2022, the Supreme Court issued a decision in *Dobbs v. Jackson Women's Health Organization* that effectively overruled *Roe v. Wade* by allowing Mississippi to ban abortions after 15 weeks of pregnancy. This decision has significant implications for the rule of law and women's access to reproductive healthcare.

With the overturning of *Roe v. Wade*, it is expected that many states will enact laws restricting access to abortion or even banning it altogether. For example, South Carolina's *Prenatal Equal Protection Act* of 2023, has made self-managed abortion illegal and seeks to make getting an abortion considered committing homicide. Inaccessibility to safe, legal abortions leads to increased rates of serious health complications and even death.[85] This also has a disproportionate impact on low-income women, who may not have the resources to travel to states where abortion is legal or to access safe and affordable healthcare. The decision to overturn *Roe v. Wade* was significant in upholding the rule of law and protecting women's right to privacy and reproductive autonomy. The overturning of the decision has significant implications for women's healthcare and their ability to make decisions about their bodies, and it highlights the ongoing struggle to balance the rights of individuals with the interests of the state.

Conclusion

The role of the judiciary in upholding the rule of law, protecting individual rights, and ensuring the proper functioning of government institutions is critical. Judges must interpret and apply laws

---

84   "Bill 3549: South Carolina Prenatal Equal Protection Act of 2023." *South Carolina General Assembly*, 10 Jan. 2023, https://www.scstatehouse.gov/sess125_2023-2024/bills/3549.html.

85   David Grimes et al, *Sexual and Reproductive Health 4: Unsafe Abortion: The Preventable Pandemic*, vol. 368, no. 9550, ser. 1908-1919, 1 Dec. 2006. *1908-1919.*

fairly and impartially, and they must be independent to ensure that they are not subject to external pressures. The case studies discussed in this chapter demonstrate how judicial decisions have upheld the rule of law and protected individual rights, setting important precedents for future cases. The judiciary is a vital component of democratic governance, and its independence and integrity must be protected.

Chapter 4: Separation of Powers

Peter Anto Johnson

Overview of the principle of separation of powers

The principle of separation of powers is one with rooted origins that hold a system of checks and balances to keep the government accountable. At its essence, it divides a nation's government into non-overlapping "branches" each with its responsibilities and roles. The most common division is known as the *trias politica*, a model where the legislative, executive, and judicial branch function to prevent the concentration of power in a government.

In his book, the Spirit of Laws, Montesquieu writes:

> "When legislative power is united with executive power in a single person or a single body of the magistracy, there is no liberty, because one can fear that the same monarch or senate that makes tyrannical laws will execute them tyrannically. Nor is there liberty if the power of judging is not separate from legislative power and executive power. If it were joined to legislative power, the power over the life and liberty of the citizens would be arbitrary, for the

judge would be the legislator. If it were joined to
executive power, the judge could have the force of
an oppressor".[86]

Importance of maintaining the separation of powers

The importance of separation of powers has been stressed on
multiple occasions in history. In his essays, Montesquieu further
elaborates on the dangers of no separation of powers. Specifically, he emphasizes the threat of a fusion of powers in a single
entity of the magistracy or monarchy denies liberty as the government will rule by fear and tyranny since they can make authoritarian legislations which can then be executed oppressively.[87]

There has never existed one system of governance without its
flaws in the history of the world, as countless forms of government with and without separation of powers have been implemented on numerous occasions yet when these measures were
not in place, we constantly see instances where innocent people
were forced to pay undeserved consequences. According to some,
it is sometimes necessary to hand over rights and liberties in exchange for a "benevolent leader", otherwise a leading assembly,
which would work for the collective good and be strong enough
to protect the security of a nation.

Thomas Hobbes' concept of the "Leviathan," reflects the very
essence of the call for the abandonment of individual rights and
freedoms for the sake of the collective.[88] Hobbes was under the

---

86   Charles Louis de Secondat Montesquieu, "Montesquieu: The
spirit of the laws" ed (Cambridge: Cambridge University Press, 1989);
Charles Louis de Secondat Montesquieu. *Persian letters*. (Oxford: Oxford University Press, 2008).

87   Jennifer Epley Sanders, "Resistance from within: Power and
defiance in Montesquieu's *Persian Letters*" (2020) 10:3 SAGE Open
215824402095155.

88   David P Gauthier, "The logic of Leviathan: the moral and
political theory of Thomas Hobbes. (Oxford: Oxford University Press,
1969).

impression that most individuals were weak and irrational, giving them individual rights and freedoms would only result in the advancement of their selfish goals that would override the collective itself. Hobbes proposed the sole way to overcome this weakness in a nation was to enable a Leviathan (the executive government in the modern context) to advance strategically and eliminate threats to security by surrendering their rights and freedoms. Jean-Jacques Rousseau was yet another huge proponent of the concept of utilitarianism within the political structure.[89]

He would agree with the ideas of Hobbes that prefer balancing the common good above individual liberties. The theory to entrust an autocratic government to guide the state to stability was supposedly a sound idea. Unfortunately, several philosophers such as John Locke, recognizing that this idea was not feasible in practice, questioned it by pointing to facts such as the aggregation of an immense political power into the hands of one or few in government.[90] Not only would this create an increased prospect for more corruption in the government, but it would also deny citizens of their rights and liberties, which Locke perceived to weigh more than the interests of the collective in society. The people who side with Locke often feel that individual rights and freedoms in a state take precedence over collective interests and sense danger in forfeiting these liberties and succumbing to autocratic rulers. Others are dependent on a responsible leader and in opposition to this idea, seeing it to be a principle of those who cling to their rights and freedoms for their self-interest and overlook larger threats in society by antagonizing the government. It becomes necessary to view liberal and democratic values as facets essential to a society, but at the same time, acknowledge temporary intervention from the government to ensure stability in the state; individuals should be granted these rights and freedoms at all times unless threatened by a state of emergency that may

---

89   Manzoor Laskar, "Summary of social contract theory by Hobbes, Locke and Rousseau." (2013) Locke and Rousseau; Jean Jacques Rousseau, Roger D Masters, & Christopher Kelly, "Rousseau Dialogues" (1990) UPNE.

90   John Fielding, "Perspectives on ideology". (Don Mills, Ont.: Oxford University Press, 2009).

require tendencies of an autocratic government to better manage the flaws of liberal democracy, but concurrently, these measures must be temporary and for the sake of public security, that does not deny basic human rights such as the right to life.

Separation of powers undermined: the Cold War

Over time, we have seen governments advance distinct ideologies, cultural values, and beliefs, which have been inconsistent from the standpoint of citizens.[91] One such occasion when views of the government collided was during the period of the Cold War between 1945 and 1991. The US headed the Western world and the Soviet Union dominated the Eastern world. Since both nations possessed nuclear weapons capable of a nuclear holocaust, most of the conflicts between the nations were proxy wars within other regions between groups indoctrinated with the Soviet Union's ideology of socialism and collectives following the liberal democratic ideology of the US. Governments made decisions autocratically. One significant event was the establishment of the Berlin Wall drawing a line between East and West Berlin. Due to the lack of separation of powers and lack of accountability of governments, the creation of this border demonstrates the Soviet Union's authoritarian government's desire to reaffirm walls that existed before the conflict. The elimination of the geographical and psychological barriers resulted in an ideological war. The overlapping of political dogmas and the lack of checks and balances led to the conflict, giving the means to proclaim one correct ideology determined by the winner.

Separation of powers undermined: German and Belgian Imperialism in Rwanda

Most importantly, the desire for power and equality incites conflict. Imperialism from the late nineteenth century to the early twentieth century has influenced several nations within the

---

91   *Ibid.*

world.[92] Under imperial rules, the monarch controlled all branches of government: judicial, legislative, and executive powers. The conquests for the expansion of colonies and power led German and Belgian imperialism to plant the seeds for bloody conflicts within the nation of Rwanda. Sprouting from supremacist approaches that deny the worth of other cultures, the German and Belgian invaders established a hierarchy in Rwanda based on biological similarities.[93] Crowning European culture as the supreme species above all else, the pyramid focused on Tutsis, a minority ethnic group within Rwanda with inherent physical features resembling stereotypical Europeans, directly below them. At the lowest level sat the Hutus, the group with the fewest physiological similarities. Until Rwanda gained independence from the imperial powers in 1962, the Hutus were socially excluded, given few privileges, and treated harshly. Without the weight of the imperial powers in the pyramid, the Hutus scrambled from under the pyramid in a revolt against the Tutsis. The Rwandan civil war from 1990 to 1993 between the Hutus and Tutsis ended the aristocracy and temporarily created a society with equality. In 1994, the assassination of the presiding Hutu representative government, Juvenal Habyarimana, ignited the genocide of billions of Tutsis. The geographical, psychological and biological wall that separated the imperialists and the lack of separation of powers in the government led to the mass massacre of the Tutsis and Hutus.

Separation of powers undermined: The War Measures Act in Canada

A contrary example where the separation of powers was forcefully but temporarily undermined in the context of a democratic government reflects the importance of the rule of law. This forceful, but temporary, intervention is seen in the *War Measures Act*, which has enforced the suspension of the individual rights and freedoms of many individuals on three occasions throughout

---

92   *Ibid.*

93   Robert Gardner & Wayne Lavold et al. "Exploring Globalization." Toronto: McGraw-Hill Ryerson, 2007. Print

Canadian history, in all cases, it was an attempt to protect public safety.[94] In the early 1960s, much of Canada and the rest of the world was undergoing momentous political, social, and cultural changes as more government control over individual affairs was loosened there were anti-war movements, women's suffrage, several efforts to end poverty, and discrimination. In Quebec, advancements were gradually being made to preserve the French language and culture by ensuring equal opportunities in employment, which was dominated by the Anglophone minority. This period was known as the Quiet Revolution where all of Canada underwent swift social, economic, and political modernization without violence or terror.

Some people, however, were displeased by the pace of change and disrupted this time of change and peace with violence, and terrorism to catalyze this process. The *Front de Liberation du Quebec* (FLQ), emerged as a terrorist and extremist group that was willing to use any means to create change in society. Throughout the period in the late 1960s, there were several extremist actions the FLQ used to express protest. The organization had several factions of supporters in society that responded in different levels of severity to protest but was most often characterized by illegal actions, acts of civil disobedience, and on the furthest end of the spectrum – terrorism. These acts of terrorism involved the bombing of several districts in Quebec and the kidnapping of integral ministers of government. In 1970, following the abduction and subsequent murder of Pierre Laporte, a British minister of trade, an enraged federal government under Pierre Trudeau made a motion for the invocation of the *War Measures Act* for a third time in Canadian history. [95]Deeming the suspension of rights and liberties, which were guaranteed by the constitution created much discontent among the citizens of Canada and Quebec. In particular, this legislation allowed for arrests based on suspicion, transforming Canada into a police state, similar to that created by Hitler. With these terms, more than 500 citizens were arrested and detained after being suspected to be potential members of the FLQ. Of these, only a few citizens were part of

94   *Ibid.*
95   *Ibid.*

the FLQ, and many people's rights to a free trial and freedoms that called for justice were largely denied.

This evoked much controversy against the federal government in Canada, yet Pierre Trudeau saw that these people were "weak-kneed," and their "bleeding hearts," in response to state control were something necessary to overlook for the sake of a greater goal. In this case, the basic human right to life was placed above rights to privacy and individual freedoms for the sake of the prevention of the several deaths that would otherwise have resulted from the actions of the FLQ. Without the actions of the government and the *War Measures Act*, it becomes clear that arrests and detainments were indeed necessary for the prevention of more deathly consequences from terrorism.

Separation of powers in the modern context: Bill C-51 in Canada

Perhaps such a system of temporary institution of authoritarian control has had a few successes; however, in a contemporary society fearful of the loss of rights just as much as terrorism, it becomes necessary to balance security such that privacy and freedom coexist despite their incompatibility. Recently, Bill C-51 also dubbed the *Anti-Terrorism Act* of 2015 was able to provoke a wave of criticism among civil rights activists.[96] One of the major clauses infringes privacy by attacking any form of expression of any ideas relating to terrorism. Endowing the government with the power to blatantly detain those alleged and suspected, while seemingly similar to Trudeau's action instead further resembles the feared authoritarian regimes in history. The core basis of this difference lies in the fact that such an act is permanent, in that once a threat has been identified and removed, the dictatorial powers provided to the government are not lifted. Instead, the threat continues to exist and will never cease due to its arbitrary definition.

---

96   Sharly Chan, "Canadian Privacy Advocacy Groups and Bill C-51". University of Toronto, 2019.

When such a large amount of power becomes aggregated in the hands of a few for an extended period solely for the sake of security, exploitation and misuse of the system become inevitable. This denial of freedom for a prolonged period rather than dealing with any threat contradicts the purpose of security. Controlling all aspects of the lives of individuals, where they can no longer freely express ideas or must be detained for the rest of their lives under the basis of suspicion would be no different from a police state or recreating the feared dictatorial regimes of history.

The flaws that exist in a liberal democracy depend on characteristics associated with totalitarian regimes, and it is only by the incorporation of both forms of government that society can respond favourably to different political circumstances. Certain facets of authoritarian rule are efficient in providing the state with security, yet the implementation of these facets must be temporary for goals to be directed towards the collective interests and not toward the selfish aims of the government. In its circadian management, the democratic values of accountability, together with individual rights and freedoms guarantee effective management during times of peace. It is only when the values of liberal democratic society are threatened by an extremist force or danger that a step towards collective security and temporary motion of illiberalism is justified for the security of the lives of citizens and the most fundamental human right to life. However, it should be stressed that such a motion is provisional and moderated.

Separation of powers in the modern context:
Harper and Senate reforms

In the autumn of 2013, the government under Prime Minister Stephen Harper submitted a set of reference questions regarding senate reform to the Supreme Court.[97] The legislation Mr. Harper was testing would require every province in Canada to enact senator-in-waiting legislation similar to the one on the books in

97   Kristin Hulme, "Alberta's Great Experiment in Senatorial Democracy". American Review of Canadian Studies, 46:1 (pp. 33-54) Routledge, Taylor & Francis Group, 2016 [*Hulme, 2016*].

Alberta at the time. The function of this legislation was to put senate candidates on the ballot any time there was a vacancy for the province in question; citizens of that province would elect a candidate and the Prime Minister would subsequently appoint that individual. Stephen Harper referred this proposed legislation to the Supreme Court because he aimed to use parliament to unilaterally alter the Senate, thus side-stepping the issue of passing a constitutional amendment which was the roadblock that sank the Charlottetown Accords and the *Meech Lake Accords*.[98] The Supreme Court, as previously mentioned, blocked this attempt to bypass constitutional amendment and offered a specific and narrow definition for the function of the Senate, primarily focusing very specifically on the complementary function of the Senate and eliminating considerations like regionality and the balance of power.

This judgment effectively halted Prime Minister Harper's attempt at Senate reform. After years of claiming that he could accomplish reform without the need for messy constitutional negotiations, the Supreme Court solidly shut the door on the possibility.[99] This interpretation of the function of the Senate speaks to the matter of legitimacy because it lends absolute clarity to the part the Senate is intended to play in the Canadian government and firmly establishes the need for a constitutional amendment to alter the role. On the topic of output, if the Senate is to be a complementary body to the House of Commons, is it not more likely that elected senators would effectively cease to function as a body of sober second thought and instead become an additional partisan forum with its own perceived mandate to govern? If this is the case it is not difficult to imagine that if the Senate finds itself with a different balance of power from the House of Commons, the upper chamber would become an obstructive body or

---

98   David C Docherty, "The Canadian Senate: Chamber of Sober Reflection or Loony Cousin Best Not Talked About". Journal of Legislative Studies, 8:3 (pp. 27-48) Routledge, Taylor & Francis Group, 2002; Herman Bakvis "Prime Minister and Cabinet in Canada: An Autocracy in Need of Reform?" Journal of Canadian Studies/Revue d'études canadiennes, 35:4 (pp. 60-79) University of Toronto Press, 2000.

99   *Hulme, 2016, supra* note 95.

that it might even actively work to undermine the efforts of the elected members of the lower chamber. For a government to be legitimate, the results of its output must be compatible with the values of the society it governs.[100] At first glance, it would appear that an elected senate would be in line with the values of Canadian society. After all, Canada is a democratic nation. This is what makes the concept of an elected senate attractive. It's certainly not a hard sell to the political body, especially when the appointed senate has felt to many as unaccountable through numerous scandals over the years. But is an elected senate the best way to achieve legitimacy?

The function of the Senate as a complementary body to the House of Commons must be taken into consideration; changes that threaten to undermine that role may also threaten the legitimacy of the Senate.[101] The trouble with electing the Senate is that if senators feel they are accountable directly to voters, they feel that they have a mandate of their own. Would creating a second democratic assembly not risk a scenario where one elected body interferes with the next? It creates a scenario where the Senate could see itself as being in competition with the House of Commons instead of being a complementary body. If the Senate is competing with the lower chamber, it is not difficult to imagine it creating dysfunction within the legislative branch as a whole. That dysfunction would certainly run counter to the values of Canadian society as expressed in the supreme court reference.[102] In considering whether a democratic senate would be in line with the values of Canadian society, we must look at the situation ho-

100   Peter G Stillman, "The Concept of Legitimacy". Polity, 7:1 (pp. 32-56) University of Chicago Press, 1974; Robert Gardner and Wayne Lavold et al. "Exploring Globalization." Toronto: McGraw-Hill Ryerson, 2007. Print.

101   Gary William O'Brien (2019) "Discovering the Senate's Fundamental Nature: Moving beyond the Supreme Court's 2014 Opinion" Canadian Journal of Political Science, 52:3 (pp. 539-555) (Cambridge: Cambridge University Press, 2019).

102   *Hulme, 2016, supra* note 95.

listically. Balancing the popular will of the people at the moment with the long-established traditions of a society is essential to determining its values.

Conclusion

The value of separation of powers and rule of law cannot be emphasized enough. On countless occasions throughout history and the contemporary era, we see recurrent themes of legitimacy and accountability of government being questioned. As such, the preservation of justice requires the acceptance that powers should not be concentrated in the hands of one individual or entity and if a situation requires it, such interventions be temporary and reversible to preserve checks and balances in the state.

Chapter 5: The Importance of Due Process

Insiya Fathima Moosavi

Overview Of Due Process

Due process refers to the legal principle that every person is entitled to fair treatment under the law and the Constitution.[103] It ensures that individuals are not deprived of their life, liberty, or property without proper legal procedures and protections. Due process includes several procedural rights, such as the right to a fair and impartial trial, the right to notice the charges against them, the right to legal representation, the right to confront and cross-examine witnesses, and the right to appeal a decision. Due process is a fundamental component of the justice system and is enshrined in the *Fifth and Fourteenth Amendments* to the U.S. Constitution.[104]

Due process is a concept that is recognized and protected in Canadian law as well.[105] In Canada, the right to due process is enshrined in Section 7 of the *Canadian Charter of Rights and*

103   Laurence H Tribe, "Structural Due Process" (1975) 10:2 *Harv CR-CL L Rev* 269–321.

104   John V Orth, *Due Process of Law: A Brief History* (University Press of Kansas, 2003) Google-Books-ID: 1yOQAAAAMAAJ.

105   F L Morton, "The Political Impact of the Canadian Charter of Rights and Freedoms" (1987) 20:1 *Canadian Journal of Political Science/Revue canadienne de science politique* 31–55.

Freedoms, which states that "everyone has the right to life, liberty and security of the person and the right not to be deprived thereof except per the principles of fundamental justice." This means that every person in Canada is entitled to certain procedural protections, such as the right to a fair and impartial trial, the right to legal representation, and the right to be informed of the charges against them. Canadian law also recognizes the principle of natural justice, which requires that decision-making processes be fair and impartial and that individuals be allowed to respond to allegations made against them. Overall, the concept of due process is an important part of the Canadian legal system and plays a critical role in ensuring that individuals are treated fairly and justly under the law.

HISTORY OF DUE PROCESS

Due process can trace its roots back to the *Magna Carta*, a charter of rights that was signed by King John of England in 1215.[106] The *Magna Carta* established the principle that everyone, including the king, was subject to the law and entitled to fair treatment under the law. It also established the right to a trial by jury, which became an important part of due process.

Over the centuries, the due process evolved as a concept and was enshrined in various legal systems around the world. In the United States, the concept of due process is enshrined in the *Fifth and Fourteenth Amendments* to the Constitution. The Fifth Amendment, ratified in 1791, provides that no person shall be deprived of life, liberty, or property without due process of law. The *Fourteenth Amendment*, ratified in 1868, extends this protection to the states.[107]

---

106   Frederick Mark Gedicks, "An Originalist Defense of Substantive Due Process: Magna Carta, Higher-Law Constitutionalism, and the Fifth Amendment" (2008) 58:3 *Emory LJ* 585–674.

107   C H McIlwain, "Due Process of Law in Magna Carta" (1914) 14:1 *Colum L Rev* 27–51.

The concept of due process has been interpreted in various ways by the courts over the years. Initially, it was seen as simply requiring notice and an opportunity to be heard. However, over time, the concept has been expanded to encompass a range of procedural and substantive rights. In the landmark case of *Palko v. Connecticut (1937)*, the Supreme Court held that some rights, such as the right to a fair trial, were so fundamental that they were incorporated into the concept of due process and applied to the states through the Fourteenth Amendment.[108]

In subsequent cases, the Supreme Court has held that due process requires that criminal defendants be provided with a range of procedural rights, such as the right to counsel, the right to a speedy trial, and the right to confront witnesses. It has also held that due process requires that laws are not arbitrary or discriminatory and that they must be clear and specific enough to provide fair notice of what is prohibited. Overall, the concept of due process has evolved to provide a comprehensive framework for ensuring fairness and justice in legal proceedings.

PROCEDURAL RIGHTS

Right to a Fair and Impartial Trial

The right to a fair and impartial trial is a fundamental component of due process and is enshrined in many national and international legal systems. This right ensures that every individual is entitled to a fair trial, regardless of their status, background, or the nature of the charges against them.[109] A fair and impartial trial is one in which the parties are given a full and fair opportunity to present their case, the proceedings are conducted according to established legal procedures, and the decision-maker is unbiased and independent. This includes the right to legal representation, the right to a public trial, the right to be informed of the charges

---

108   Richard Polenberg, "Cardozo and the Criminal Law: Palko v. Connecticut Reconsidered" (1996) 1996:2 *J Sup Ct Hist* 92–105.

109   Lewis F Powell, "The Right to a Fair Trial" (1965) 51:6 *American Bar Association Journal* 534–538.

against them, and the right to confront and cross-examine witnesses. The right to a fair and impartial trial is a critical component of the justice system and is essential for ensuring that justice is done in every case. It promotes public confidence in the legal system and helps to prevent wrongful convictions or other miscarriages of justice.

Right to Notice of the Charges Against

The right to notice the charges against an individual is a fundamental aspect of due process and is often referred to as the "right to be informed" or "right to know." This right ensures that individuals are aware of the specific charges or allegations against them and have the opportunity to prepare a defence.[110] The right to notice the charges against an individual includes a requirement that the charges be stated with sufficient clarity and detail to enable the accused to understand the nature of the accusations and the evidence that will be presented against them. This right also includes the right to be informed of any potential consequences or penalties that may result from a conviction. The right to notice the charges against an individual is essential to protecting individual rights and ensuring a fair trial. It enables the accused to prepare a defence and challenge the evidence presented by the prosecution. It also promotes transparency and accountability in the legal system and helps to prevent abuses of power and wrongful convictions.

Right to Legal Representation

The right to legal representation is a fundamental aspect of due process and is often referred to as the "right to counsel." This right ensures that individuals who are facing criminal charges or other legal proceedings can obtain the assistance of a qualified

---

110   Tara Ward, "The Right to Free, Prior, and Informed Consent: Indigenous Peoples' Participation Rights within International Law" (2011) 10:2 *Nw U J Int'l Hum Rts* 54–84.

lawyer to represent their interests.[111] The right to legal representation includes a requirement that individuals have access to legal counsel at all stages of the legal process, including during questioning, pre-trial proceedings, and trial. This right also includes the right to have an attorney present during any interactions with law enforcement or other government officials. The right to legal representation is essential to protecting individual rights and ensuring a fair trial. It enables individuals to understand their legal rights and options, navigate the legal system, and mount a vigorous defence against the charges they are facing. It also promotes fairness and impartiality in the legal system and helps to prevent abuses of power and wrongful convictions.

Right to Confront and Cross-Examine Witnesses

The right to confront and cross-examine witnesses is a fundamental aspect of due process and is enshrined in many national and international legal systems. This right ensures that individuals who are facing criminal charges or other legal proceedings have the opportunity to challenge the evidence presented against them by the prosecution.[112] The right to confront and cross-examine witnesses includes the right to question witnesses who are called to testify against the accused. This right also includes the right to present evidence in their defence and to have witnesses testify on their behalf. This right is essential to protecting individual rights and ensuring a fair trial. It enables individuals to challenge the credibility and accuracy of the evidence presented against them and to present their version of events. It also promotes transparency and accountability in the legal system and helps to prevent abuses of power and wrongful convictions.

---

111   Mary Sue Backus and Paul Marcus, "The Right to Counsel in Criminal Cases, a National Crisis" (2005) 57:6 *Hastings LJ* 1031–1130.

112   Daniel H Pollitt, "The Right of Confrontation: Its History and Modern Dress" (1959) 8:2 *J Pub L* 381–413.

Right to Appeal a Decision

The right to appeal a decision is a fundamental aspect of due process and is often referred to as the "right to appeal". This right ensures that individuals who are dissatisfied with a decision made in a legal proceeding have the opportunity to challenge that decision before a higher court or authority.[113] The right to appeal a decision includes the right to request a review of the legal proceedings that led to the decision, as well as the right to challenge the legal reasoning and factual findings that underlie the decision. This right also includes the right to present new evidence that was not available at the time of the original proceeding. The right to appeal a decision is essential to protecting individual rights and ensuring a fair legal system. It enables individuals to challenge decisions that they believe are unjust or incorrect and provides a mechanism for correcting errors and ensuring that justice is done. It also promotes transparency and accountability in the legal system and helps to prevent abuses of power and wrongful convictions.

Importance Of Due Process in Upholding the Rule of Law

The rule of law is a fundamental principle that underpins democratic societies and refers to the idea that everyone is subject to the law, including those who govern. It is a system where laws are consistently and fairly applied, and no one is above the law. The rule of law means that decisions are made according to established laws and procedures, rather than based on personal whim or arbitrary decision-making. It requires that laws be clear and publicly available and that they be enforced equally and impartially. The rule of law also includes the principle of judicial independence, which means that judges are free to make decisions based on the law and the facts of the case, without fear of political interference or retribution.

---

113   Cassandra Burke Robertson, "The Right to Appeal" (2012) 91:4 *NC L Rev* 1219–1282.

Due process is critical to upholding the rule of law because it provides the procedural protections necessary to ensure that the law is applied fairly and impartially. Without due process, the rule of law would be undermined, and individuals could be subjected to arbitrary or unjust treatment by the government or other powerful entities. By ensuring that individuals are given notice of the charges against them, the opportunity to present evidence and witnesses in their defence, and the right to a fair and impartial hearing, the due process helps to safeguard against wrongful convictions and other miscarriages of justice. Furthermore, the principles of due process help to ensure that the law is applied equally and consistently, without favour or discrimination. This promotes public confidence in the justice system and helps to prevent abuses of power by those in positions of authority.

Overall, due process is essential to upholding the rule of law and serves as a key safeguard against tyranny, injustice, and the arbitrary exercise of power.

Case Studies of Countries Where Due Process Has Been Violated

The following case studies describe landmark decisions in Canada's Supreme Court that upheld the principle of due process in the country's justice system. They helped set the precedent of due process for all future legal cases in Canada and serve as important cornerstones to the legal system. These case studies were pulled from the Government of Canada website.[114]

---

114   Department of Justice Government of Canada, "Examples of Charter-related cases - Canada's Sytem of Justice" (12 April 2018) online: *Government of Canada* <https://www.justice.gc.ca/eng/csj-sjc/rfc-dlc/ccrf-ccdl/cases.html> Last Modified: 2022-04-05.

R. V. STINCHCOMBE[115]

R. v. Stinchcombe is a landmark decision by the Supreme Court of Canada that has had a significant impact on criminal law in Canada. The case involved the duty of the Crown (prosecution) to disclose all relevant evidence to the defence in criminal trials. The accused in the case, David Stinchcombe, was charged with possession of a narcotic for trafficking. During his trial, he requested disclosure of all evidence in the Crown's possession that was relevant to his case. The Crown provided some of the requested evidence but withheld other evidence that is deemed not to be relevant.

The Supreme Court of Canada, in a unanimous decision, held that the Crown has a constitutional duty to disclose all relevant evidence to the defence in criminal trials. The Court found that the Crown's duty to disclose is grounded in the accused's right to a fair trial and the principle of full answer and defence. The Court emphasized that the Crown must disclose all evidence, whether it is incriminating or exculpatory, and that it is not up to the Crown to decide what evidence is relevant or not. The Crown must also disclose all evidence promptly, and failure to disclose can result in the exclusion of evidence or even a stay of proceedings.

The decision in *Stinchcombe* has had a significant impact on criminal law in Canada, as it has established a clear and comprehensive framework for the disclosure of evidence in criminal trials. It has also led to a greater emphasis on the principle of fairness in criminal proceedings and has helped to ensure that accused persons can fully exercise their right to make full answers and defences.

The decision in *R. v. Stinchcombe* is closely related to the concept of due process in Canadian criminal law. Due process requires that an accused person be provided with a fair trial, and this includes the right to full disclosure of all relevant evidence in the possession of the prosecution. In Stinchcombe, the Supreme Court of Canada recognized that the duty of the Crown to dis-

---

115   Lexum, "R. v. Stinchcombe - SCC Cases" online: *Lexum* <https://scc-csc.lexum.com/scc-csc/scc-csc/en/item/808/index.do>.

close all relevant evidence to the defence is grounded in the accused's right to a fair trial and the principle of full answer and defence. This duty of disclosure is a fundamental aspect of due process in Canadian criminal law. By requiring the prosecution to disclose all relevant evidence to the defence, the *Stinchcombe* decision ensures that the accused person can make a full answer and defence to the charges against them. This helps to ensure that the trial is fair and that the accused person's rights are protected.

NEW BRUNSWICK (MINISTER OF HEALTH AND COMMUNITY SERVICES) V. G. (J.)[116]

The case of *New Brunswick (Minister of Health and Community Services) v. G. (J.)* is an important decision by the Supreme Court of Canada that is closely related to the concept of due process. In the case of Ms. G and her children, the New Brunswick Minister of Health and Community Services took custody of her three children for six months and sought an extension for another six months. Ms. G, who was unable to afford a lawyer, was denied legal aid when she applied under New Brunswick's Domestic Legal Aid Program. She argued that the program violated her right to security of the person because she would not have a fair hearing without legal representation. The Supreme Court agreed, ruling that parents have the right to a fair hearing in custody cases and that this may require legal representation if the case involves complex facts or legal arguments, and the parent cannot afford a lawyer. This case established that parents who challenge a government agency's removal of their child from their care have the right to meaningfully participate in the custody hearing and confirmed that the Charter's protection of the right to life, liberty, and security of the person applies not only to criminal law cases.

New Brunswick (Minister of Health and Community Services) v. G. (J.), [1999] 3 SCR 46 is an important decision by the Supreme Court of Canada related to the concept of due process. The case

---

116   Lexum, "New Brunswick (Minister of Health and Community Services) v. G. (J.) - SCC Cases" online: *Lexum* <https://scc-csc.lexum.com/scc-csc/scc-csc/en/item/1725/index.do>.

involved a challenge to the constitutionality of a provision in the New Brunswick Family Services Act that allowed the government to remove children from their parents without a court order in certain circumstances. The Supreme Court held that the provision was unconstitutional because it violated the principles of fundamental justice, which are a key aspect of due process. The Court found that the provision violated the principles of fundamental justice by denying parents their right to a fair hearing before an impartial decision-maker, which is a fundamental principle of justice protected by the Canadian *Charter of Rights and Freedoms*.

The case involved a challenge to the constitutionality of a provision in the New Brunswick Family Services Act that allowed the government to remove children from their parents without a court order in certain circumstances. The Supreme Court of Canada held that the provision was unconstitutional because it violated the principles of fundamental justice, which are a key aspect of due process. The Court held that the provision violated the principles of fundamental justice because it deprived parents of their right to a fair hearing before an impartial decision-maker. The Court noted that the right to a fair hearing is an essential aspect of the rule of law and is a fundamental principle of justice that is protected by the Canadian *Charter of Rights and Freedoms*.

The decision in *New Brunswick (Minister of Health and Community Services) v. G. (J.)* is significant because it reinforces the importance of due process in protecting individual rights and ensuring a fair and just legal system. The decision emphasizes the need for procedural fairness and the importance of impartial decision-making in legal proceedings.

R V. JORDAN[117]

The *R v. Jordan* trial was a landmark decision by the Supreme Court of Canada concerning the right to trial within a reasonable

---

117   Lexum, "R. v. Jordan - SCC Cases" online: *Lexum* <https://scc-csc.lexum.com/scc-csc/scc-csc/en/item/16057/index.do>.

time, which is a crucial aspect of due process in criminal trials. Barrett Jordan, who was charged with drug-related offences in 2008, was convicted in 2013 after a delay of more than 49 months. Jordan argued that the delay violated his right to a timely trial, and the Supreme Court agreed, establishing new guidelines to determine reasonable or unreasonable delays. The Court's decision set a default timeline of 18 months for cases tried in provincial court and 30 months for cases tried in superior court. Exceptions to these timelines would only be made in exceptional circumstances. The Court emphasized that undue delay negatively affects not only the accused but also the victims of the crime and society's interest in justice.

This trial is also closely related to the concept of due process. The case involved a challenge to the right to trial within a reasonable time, which is a key aspect of due process in criminal trials. The accused in the case, Barrett Jordan, was charged with drug trafficking and other offences. The trial was delayed for several years due to various issues, including delays in disclosure and scheduling conflicts. The case eventually made its way to the Supreme Court of Canada, which held that the right to trial within a reasonable time had been violated in this case. The Court set out a new framework for determining whether a delay in a criminal trial is unreasonable and violates an accused person's right to trial within a reasonable time. The Court held that there is a presumptive ceiling of 18 months between the time of an accused person's charge and the anticipated end of a trial in provincial court cases, and 30 months for cases tried in superior court. The Court's decision in *R v. Jordan* emphasizes the importance of timely justice in upholding the principles of due process. The right to trial within a reasonable time is a fundamental aspect of due process because it ensures that accused persons are not subject to undue delays and that justice is served in a timely and efficient manner. Overall, the decision in *R v. Jordan* underscores the importance of due process in criminal trials and emphasizes the need for timely justice to ensure that accused persons can exercise their rights and that justice is served fairly and efficiently.

Conclusion

In conclusion, the concept of due process is an essential concept in North American law that helps uphold a fair and accessible justice system. It has a long and dynamic history that informs the continual development and refinement of how due process is understood in contemporary courts. Due process encompasses key procedural rights, including the right to a fair and impartial trial, a notice of charges against, legal counsel, confront and cross-examine witnesses, and the right to appeal a decision. Through landmark cases presented in front of the Canadian Supreme Court, this chapter highlighted the importance of due process in upholding the rule of law.

Chapter 6: Access to Justice

Meera Chawda

Importance of Access to Justice in Upholding the Rule of Law

The rule of law provides a foundational governance upon which a country functions in a well-ordered manner. The rule of law applies to every person functioning under the governance, including citizens and lawmakers alike. In this chapter, access to justice in upholding the rule of law will be scrutinized on an international and national scale. Barriers will be considered in accessing justice along with possible solutions. Moreover, the role of legal aid will be discussed relating to accessing justice. Finally, case studies will be presented involving countries where access to justice has been restricted.

According to the UN, access to justice is a basic principle of the rule of law as it ensures that citizens' rights are protected and exercised and lawmakers are held accountable if there are any defiances.[118] Within Canada, access to justice is considered a fundamental value to the Canadian justice system as evidenced by Sustainable Development Goal 16 which states that the rule of law must work to "promote peaceful and inclusive societies

---

118   United Nations, "Access to justice - united nations and the rule of law" (n.d.) online: *United Nations* <https://www.un.org/ruleoflaw/thematic-areas/access-to-justice-and-rule-of-law-institutions/access-to-justice/> [*UN, n.d.*].

for sustainable development, provide access to justice for all, and build effective, accountable, and inclusive institutions at all levels".[119] Access to justice is often assumed to just include the ability of a citizen to seek assistance through formal justice systems.[120] However, it is important to note that informal forms of receiving justice in developing countries are also a form of seeking justice and maybe just as instrumental in disadvantaged groups' perceptions of access to justice. Legal issues do not occur in isolation; they are often embedded with intersecting problems relating to housing, employment, education and health which risk the livelihoods of economically disadvantaged individuals.[121] Thus, access to justice generally encompasses providing legal protection, legal awareness, legal aid and counsel, adjudication, enforcement, and civil society oversight.[122] In theory, equitable access to justice must involve vulnerable groups and must not discriminate against people of colour, gender, age, religion, status, and more.

Despite efforts to uphold these values, there are plenty of shortcomings related to the accessibility of justice for citizens globally and nationally. For example, globally, more than 5 billion people lack meaningful access to justice.[123] Barriers to justice include a lack of information and availability of services, the financial cost of legal aid, literacy, disability, geographical location, time

119   Government of Canada, Department of Justice, "Access to justice" (1 September 2021) online: *Government of Canada, Department of Justice, Electronic Communications* <https://www.justice.gc.ca/eng/csj-sjc/access-acces/index.html> [*Gov Canada, 2021*].

120   United Nations, "Strengthening Judicial Integrity through Enhanced Access to Justice" (2004) online: *United Nations Development Programme* <https://www.undp.org/sites/g/files/zskgke326/files/publications/Justice_PN_En.pdf> [*UN, 2004*].

121   Vladyslav Teremetskyi, Yevheniia Duliba, Olena Drozdova, Liudmyla Zhukovska, Olena Sivash & Iurii Dziuba, "Access to justice and legal aid for vulnerable groups: new challenges caused by the COVID-19 pandemic" (2021) 1:11 *Journal of Legal, Ethical and Regulatory Issues* 24 [*Teremetskyi et al.*].

122   *UN, 2004, supra* note 3 at 14.

123   *Gov Canada, 2021, supra* note 2 at para 4.

and complexity of cases to provide justice, and other diverse needs that may not be met.[124] Furthermore, marginalized groups such as migrants, refugees, and detainees may also be exposed to prejudice secondary to access to justice which may exacerbate issues relating to justice. With an added layer of the COVID-19 pandemic, economically disadvantaged individuals have been disproportionately affected, impacting the standard of living. For instance, the availability of justice services may have been withheld due to social distancing, which may not have been curbed due to the lack of availability of technology.[125]

With these barriers, established solutions have included social services, family services, legal aid, and other restorative justice programs to help victims deal with the aftermath of crimes. Without systems in place to provide access to justice, the rule of law may face breakdowns as citizens may not receive recourse and feel disempowered in claiming their rights, thus creating negative repercussions in the overall governance of law.

The Role of Legal Aid in Ensuring Access to Justice

An important part of providing access to justice includes ensuring legal aid for individuals to help present their cases in a costly justice system. In addition to promoting access to justice for economically disadvantaged individuals, legal aid ensures that marginalized groups and individuals are not discriminated against, are not socially excluded and public confidence in the justice system is upheld. Economically disadvantaged individuals may seek legal aid relating to issues with consumerism, crime, employment and disability, social security, debt payment, housing, domestic violence, property ownership and personal injury. Furthermore, a key approach by governmental institutions to increasing legal aid involves providing legal empowerment through educational campaigns, counselling, and legal agencies that aim to improve trust in the judicial process.[126] Legal empowerment can enhance

124   *Ibid* at para 10.

125   *UN, 2004, supra* note 5 at para 11.

126   *Teremetskyi et al., supra* note 4 at 811.

the capacity of disadvantaged groups to help them exercise their rights, assisting them to move towards justice. However, the cost of legal advice and representation has still been identified as a major obstacle to accessing justice.[127]

According to the United Nations, there is no specific delivery model of legal aid, however, a recommendation does exist that countries must consider the best model and its implications. Main delivery systems may include university law clinics, specialized legal aid service providers, public defenders, private lawyers, and paralegal schemes. Public defender schemes include legal advice and assistance provided by lawyers funded by national or civil society organizations. Private lawyer schemes involve legal aid services provided by licensed lawyers working in private firms. They may also participate in "judiciary", state-funded legal aid on a case-by-case basis. Paralegal schemes feature paralegal professionals who perform some functions of lawyers but are not autonomous to perform all functions. University law clinics involve law students supervised by lawyers and law professors, while specialized service providers provide legal aid for certain socio-demographic groups. This may involve marginalized groups such as women, children, detainees, and more to defend their individual needs.[128] While these services may exist, the allocation of a sufficient budget for legal aid is often a concern for countries. For instance, budgets for legal aid may not consider the full range of services available which may limit access to these services. Furthermore, institutions may not be able to meet the demand for lawyers due to shortages of qualified lawyers and appropriate training for individual services.

Legal aid must be provisioned to ensure that standards are upheld for principles such as equity. A partnership between regulatory bodies and legal aid authorities is established and varies in its

---

127   *UN, n.d., supra* note 1 at 5.

128   United Nations Office on Drugs and Crime, "Handbook on Ensuring Quality of Legal Aid Services in Criminal Justice Processes" (2019) online: *United Nations* <https://www.unodc.org/documents/justice-and-prison-reform/20-00556_Handbook_Legal_Aid_Ebook.pdf> [*UN, 2019*].

manifestation across countries.[129] For instance, in Canada, legal services are provisioned by the lawyer's licensing body, bar associations and legal aid plan. In countries such as France, Belgium and Germany, bar associations ensure the general quality of legal services and handle complaints for breaches. In contrast, South Africa has an independent unit called the Legal Quality Assurance Unit (LQAU) to provision the integrity of legal services.

Case Studies of Countries Where Access to Justice Has Been Restricted

In *Abdelrazik v. Canada,* the case study features a Canadian citizen, Abousfian Abdelrazik reportedly had his name wrongfully added to various anti-terrorism lists and was tortured by Sudanese officials during his visit to back-home to Sudan[130]. After his imprisonment in Sudan, the Canadian government restricted his ability to return to Canada and left him without any means of support. A year later, Sudanese authorities released Abdelrazik from detention and he made his return to Canada with many barriers such as commercial airlines refusing entry into their flying list. Later on, Abdelrazik was summoned to meet the Sudanese authorities, was re-arrested and detained for further nine months before he was re-released once again. With many incidents occurring over the next few years between Abdelrazik, the Canadian and Sudanese governments and the United Nations, Canada's Federal Court found that his rights had been violated according to the Canadian Charter of Rights and Freedoms[131]. Abdelrazik was released to return home through the help of pro bono counselling he was able to receive to win this Charter litigation. However, this issue raised various concerns regarding the safety and security of his family and life after receiving justice. The mistreatment of this Canadian citizen abroad displays how Canadians, despite

---

129   *Ibid* at para 3.

130   Sean Rehaag, "Restricted access to justice for Canadians mistreated abroad: Abdelrazik v Canada (re: Interim costs)" (2011) 29 *Windsor Yearbook of Access to Justice* 225.

131   *Ibid* at 227.

living in a developed country, may be vulnerable and experience injustice when travelling abroad. Additionally, the intense public and international nature of the issue allowed for pro bono counselling which enabled justice. This is always the case involving marginalized individuals, who may not receive pro bono counselling due to the acuity of the case, lack of media attention, and funding. Thus, *Abdelrazik v Canada* illuminates the importance of receiving access to justice through legal aid and support even when Canadian citizens are outside of Canada.

As aforementioned in this chapter, access to justice can take many forms: access to courts, legal information, education, legal aid, legal representation and other services to empower individuals. A particular population that has continued to face challenges in accessing justice globally are women. For instance, in many African communities, women continue to struggle with receiving justice for the deprivation of their rights to no avail. Moreover, access to justice for women has had significant impacts on the public health of women in specific regions and populations[132]. In statistics, African women continue to bear the greatest burden of reproduction issues evidenced by a high HIV prevalence, lack of contraception availability and education, unlawful abortions, higher incidences of sexual violence and maternal mortality rates[133]. While these statistics are saddening, it is conspicuous that access to justice in the form of education, empowerment and treatment plays a key role in public health. In a study conducted by Cai and researchers, studies showed that institutional discrimination against women in low and middle-income countries manifested in formal and informal lows led to a higher rate of suicide mortality[134]. These institutional discrimination patterns manifested as women having limited access to financial assets,

---

132   Ziyi Cai et al, "Women's suicide in low-, middle-, and high-income countries: Do laws discriminating against women matter?" (2021) 282 *Social Science & Medicine* 114035.

133   Michelle Rufaro Maziwisa & Ebenezer Durojaye, "Engendering legal and institutional reforms to ensure access to reproductive justice for women in Zimbabwe: A case study of the mapingure case" (2022) 30:1 *African Journal of International and Comparative Law* 80.

134   *Ibid* 15 at 6.

unequal rights in family law regarding divorce and inheritance, and restricted access to civil liberties. For instance, populations, where women had unequal citizenship rights or limited access to justice, saw higher suicide ratios compared to men. Thus, these findings are significant as they illuminate the impact of access to justice on population health and well-being.

A case study to exemplify the lack of access to female reproductive justice is *Mapingure v. Minister of Home Affairs*[135]. In 2006, Mapingure from Zimbabwe was attacked and raped within the boundaries of her own home. Immediately following this event, Mapingure sought assistance from the medical services available to prevent pregnancy and relevant sexually transmitted infections. However, the medical practitioner denied assistance with preventing pregnancy as they would need police presence and only within 72 hours of the rape. Mapingure rushed to receive help from the police, only to find that the constable in charge of her case was not available. Mapingure returned to convey this information to her medical practitioner and urged her to help as it was nearing 72 hours of her rape, which would otherwise result in an unplanned pregnancy. Three days following the rape, Mapingure finally received assistance from a police officer who would offer his presence to the medical practitioner. Unfortunately, at that time 72 hours had elapsed, and the medical practitioner reported that she could not be treated. A month later, Mapingure was confirmed pregnant. To receive assistance to terminate the pregnancy thereafter, the prosecution office informed her that she would need an order. After finally receiving the pregnancy termination order which took months, the hospital matron who was assigned to carry out the procedure felt that it was no longer safe to go through with the surgery and declined. Mapingure was forced to carry out the pregnancy and gave birth later that December. Upon escalating her concern to various levels of court, the Supreme Court decision held that the police and doctor failed to carry out their professional duties to avert the pregnancy. While other parties were also held liable and accountable, it is conspicuous that timely assistance was not delivered, resulting in poor health outcomes. Moreover, access to justice could have played a key

135   *Ibid* 15 at 81.

role in preventing unplanned pregnancies and altering the course of Mapingure's life. The denial of legally available services such as abortion care can cause tremendous long-lasting physical and emotional suffering, and can often be amounted to a traumatic experience[136]. Along with the burden of raising an unplanned child, Mapingure would be further stigmatized in her society for the events that occurred to her. This case study serves as an important occurrence that having low social status in society can often create barriers to seeking justice. Access to justice is a key component to upholding the rule of law and can act as a catalyst to achieve gender equality.

The American College of Obstetricians and Gynecologists v. United States Food and Drug Administration case study exemplifies the restricted access to medical abortion during COVID-19 which potentially threatened women's reproductive rights[137]. In an unprecedented time, such as the COVID-19 pandemic, physical and social distancing measures were put into place, changing the accessibility of many services across the globe. Two drugs, known as mifepristone and misoprostol, are a part of the medical abortion regimen in the United States. The approval process for dispensing the drug involves in-person interventions and signature requirements to ensure appropriate handling. However, during the pandemic, this in-person requirement was unable to be fulfilled due to public health measures. The American College of Obstetricians and Gynecologists challenged this imposition as it created barriers for women to access justice for their reproductive rights. The ruling, however, was not granted. At present, the Supreme Court has deferred any ruling until each state court modifies its requirements. Thus, eighteen states out of fifty within the United States restrict the use of telemedicine provisions for abortion services[138]. This ongoing case serves as an important remind-

136   *Ibid* 15 at 83.

137   Christina Fuleihan, "American college of obstetricians and gynecologists v. United States Food & Drug Administration Restricted access to medical abortion threatens reproductive rights during the covid-19 pandemic" (2020) 46:4 *American Journal of Law & Medicine* 507.

138   *Ibid* at 516.

er that while developing countries may make strides in promoting access to justice, the same developing countries also continue to face challenges in providing actual accessibility resources.

Race continues to play a relevant factor in the level of access to justice across the world. More specifically, the anti-Haitian bias in the Dominican Republic continues to act as a barrier to the Black population's inclusion[139]. *Yean and Bocio v. the Dominican Republic* exhibited the discrimination Black individuals face living within the Dominican Republic and has had expansive effects on identity, citizenship and access to public education. For context, the country's strained relationship with Haiti has manifested Dominican citizens' distaste for the Haitian skin colour which continues to pervade the institutional mechanisms. Consequently, individuals with a Blacker complexion are forced to overcome their skin tone to receive the same education provided to Dominican citizens. This problematic institutional system has a profound impact on access to justice and access to education plays a large role in individuals feeling empowered and autonomous. For instance, in *Yean and Bocio v. Dominican Republic,* mothers of Haitian-ancestry children requested birth certificates from the Dominican civil registry. After presenting documents that they were indeed born in the Dominican Republic, the registry refused to issue a birth certificate, claiming to deny their Dominican nationality. Although the mothers of Yean and Boscio continued to appeal this claim to the judicial system, the refusal was upheld which led to Boscio's expulsion from school[140]. Unfortunately, institutional discrimination regarding citizenship continues to play a large factor in whether individuals of Haitian complexion receive education, access to resources and other fundamental human rights. This case study, once again, serves as an example of access to justice being repeatedly denied and where the rule of law is not upheld.

139　Sheridan Wigginton, "Blackness as a barrier to citizenship and education: Situating the example of Dilcia Yean and Violeta Bosico" (2010) 5:2 *Education, Citizenship and Social Justice* 163.

140　*Ibid* at 66.

The Path Forward: Improving Access to Justice

Increasing access to justice has immense benefits for society as a whole as it can improve social cohesion and enhance people's well-being. Community-based solutions have been recommended to help improve access to justice and enhance equity. A major step towards improving qualification would be to increase inclusion criteria for legal aid and assistance. This can be done with the support of regulators within governmental funding to increase the reach of individuals who may need assistance to access justice. Another solution includes continuous and increasing pro bono contributions by lawyers and organizations. This will not only enhance access to justice but also inspire other organizations to do the same. Moreover, with the involvement of law students, pro bono work can play an instrumental role in providing relevant experience in their fields. Finally, law curriculums can be enhanced by providing educational modules on the intersection of justice and emerging fields of genetics, sociology and biology[141]. For instance, law modules can take into account mental health issues, conducting meaningful self-evaluation, and other topics that continue to play a role in the topic of access to justice. Furthermore, relevant topics relating to the political climate will allow law students to work with real-life examples. With the support of government and organizations, increasing access to justice will have profound impacts on the population's well-being and the rule of law being upheld.

Conclusion

Through the aforementioned information, access to justice is a key aspect of upholding the rule of law. Without access to justice, individuals who may encounter injustices within the confines of society may express scepticism about the justice system resulting in the breakdown of the rule of law. Through the revisions of case studies, it is conspicuous that developed and developing countries alike and individuals of marginalized groups often experience

---

141   Fatos Selita, "Improving access to justice: Community-Based Solutions" (2019) 6:1-2 *Asian Journal of Legal Education* 83.

inaccessibility to justice, and thus, suffer disproportionately compared to other populations. For instance, in *Abdelrazik v. Canada*,
the importance of receiving legal aid and timely support to individuals living outside of Canada was highlighted. Another case
study as seen in *Mapingure v. Minister of Home Affairs* showed
that multiple bodies of institutions may be involved in denying or
being negligent in providing access to justice. It is also important
to note that access to justice may be limited for citizens living
in both developed and developing countries and thus, remains a
global issue for consideration. Solutions to mobilizing access to
justice include increasing legal aid amounts, it may be important
to consider alternative solutions to receive justice. For instance,
alternative dispute mechanisms that are non-judicial institutions
may involve customary law, community arbitration and more
can increase accessibility, and social representation and provide
predictable outcomes (Ref 4). This alternative solution can be just
as effective for economically disadvantaged individuals and less
costly as they bypass traditional legal systems such as the court.
However, governments of various countries must ensure that key
citizen rights such as justice, autonomy and freedom are maintained within this practice. As a global system moving towards
seeking and establishing equity, government structures must
empower individuals to receive justice through various avenues
as this will contribute towards upholding the rule of law.

Chapter 7: Donoghue v Stevenson: A Landmark Case

Bilal Ahmed

This chapter covers an overview and introductory analysis of the *Donoghue v. Stevenson* case that took place in Scotland in 1932. The outcome of this case, as will be discussed, brought about drastic changes in laws of the negligence of care that can be seen today in the common law. [142] This chapter will begin with an introduction to the concept of landmark cases, followed by an overview of the case itself. Following this, the case will be analyzed for its implications on how to define the duty of care in common law, and how these implications have spread globally.

The Role of Landmark Cases in Law

The judicial system is designed to provide predictable and just outcomes whenever a legal issue arises. Whenever possible, courts will make their best efforts to keep consistency in how the law is interpreted. Given that most of Canada operate on a common law system, this consistency of rulings is achieved through the fact that a common law court should adhere to the <u>precedent of any</u> case decided before it. Although laws try to be

142   All Answers Ltd, "Donoghue v Stevenson [1932] Doctrine of negligence" (April 2023) online: *LawTeacher.net* <https://www.law-teacher.net/cases/donoghue-v-stevenson.php?vref=1>.

as comprehensive as possible, there are inevitable instances in which novel cases require extrapolation of the law from judges.[143] In these landmark cases, there are no formal "new laws" that are written by the judicial system, though the precedent is important nonetheless since it gives other courts an idea of how they should go about those unique situations, or situations epistemologically connected to them.

As a simple example, one could have a law that states that stealing apples from a store is considered shoplifting and that shoplifting is a punishable crime. One day, an apple accidentally falls into a customer's basket, who leaves the store with the apple unknowingly, without paying for it. In this case, while the shop owner can file a lawsuit against the customer for theft, greater deliberation must be made by the court to see if the customer is found to be guilty— and if so, the court must provide a full process that was followed to come to that conclusion. In this case, the judge must first be aware of decisions made on any similar hearings that were done in a higher court. This is to stay consistent with past decisions, a principle which is referred to as *stare decisis*.[144] If a case is presented in court, that means it is a possible scenario, and even if it has not happened in the past, it may certainly happen again in the future. In this scenario, if there have never been any prior cases in the history of said "accidental shoplifting", one must look upon the periphery of common law to extrapolate a decision. In this scenario, the hypothetical outcome may be that the defendant is found not guilty because although they shoplifted, they performed it unintentionally and thus were not liable for the act of chance that made the apple fall into their basket. This case would hence be referred to as a "landmark case"— not only would it set a precedent for other similar cases and how their outcomes will look in the future, but it also adds to the common law such that courts can use it to infer new details

---

143   Brendan Scullion, "What is a landmark case?" (18 January 2023) online: *Constitution of the United State s*<https://constitutionus.com/law/what-is-a-landmark-case/>.

144   Julie Young, "Stare decisis: What it means in law, with examples" (22 November 2022) online: *Investopedia* <https://www.investopedia.com/terms/s/stare_decisis.asp>.

on the rights of the individual as they relate to any other case. For example, this hypothetical apple case would demonstrate that a person is less culpable of a bad action when lacking a bad intent, which may be used as a factor in deciding upon other cases where a person did not have bad intent, even if it may have little to do with apples or shoplifting.

Finally, where an original precedent is presently seen as being harmful or deconstructive, it must then be overturned to create a better precedent that can be adhered to. Landmark cases can be overturned by other landmark cases.[145]

To conclude this section, beyond the laws governing a country, landmark cases can influence a person's daily life, and the way a government operates, and can even have international influence depending on how much traction the case receives. *Donoghue v. Stevenson* is a fantastic example of a case that has affected many of these facets, which is expected of a case that speaks to society's current understanding of the rights of the individual and how they can be upheld.

An Overview of Donoghue vs. Stevenson

Donoghue vs. Stevenson is often called the "Paisley Snail" or "Snail in the Bottle" case and covers an incident in which May Donoghue fell ill due to the sight of a decomposed snail in her ginger beer. The case took place on May 26th, 1932, though it continues to be relevant even to this day.[146] The case called into question the exact boundaries of what is considered culpable negligence on behalf of a seller, with or without a contractual relationship with another person.

On August 26th, 1928, May Donoghue went to a cafe with her friend, where her friend ordered a ginger beer for Ms. Donoghue

---

145   *Ibid*; *supra* note 2.

146   Stanley Buckmaster et al, "United Kingdom House of Lords Decisions: Donoghue v Stevenson [1932] UKHL 100" (1932) online: *BAILii* <https://www.bailii.org/uk/cases/UKHL/1932/100.html>.

as well as an item for herself. The ginger beer that Donoghue's friend ordered was supposedly manufactured by Stevenson, the respondent. Since the beer was served in an opaque bottle, and the bottle was sealed before serving, neither Ms. Donoghue, her friend, nor the shopkeeper was able to inspect or discern before-hand that there might have been a snail inside the bottle.[147] Ms. Donoghue drank most of the bottle and only realized that there was a snail inside when the final remnants of the bottle were poured out into a tumbler. Ms. Donoghue consulted a doctor and was diagnosed with shock and severe gastroenteritis.[148]

During the common law proceeding, many relevant cases such as *Francis v. Cockrell, George v. Skivington*, and *Winterbottom v. Wright* were brought up, though these cases provided an incomplete set of references for the case at hand, for a few reasons. Firstly, the tort in question was merely due to negligence, and not due to fraud or any other action of deliberate intent. Secondly, the plaintiff did not have any direct relationship with the manufacturer, given that the manufacturer distributed the bottle first to a retailer, who then sold it to Donoghue's friend, who gave it to her to drink. These two factors created a unique case in which no cases could be referenced where the seller knew they were selling faulty products, or where the plaintiff had been the one who bought the product.[149]

Furthermore, unlike cases such as *Dominion Natural Gas Co. Ltd. v. Collins & Perkins*, where the product (i.e., natural gas) is known to be dangerous and thus should be inspected with an added degree of care, ginger beer is not known to be innately dangerous. [150]

---

147   *Ibid.*

148   Rocco Neglia, "Donoghue v. Stevenson" (31 January 2019) online: *Canadian Underwriter* <https://www.canadianunderwriter.ca/features/cc-donoghue-v-stevenson/>.

149   All Answers ltd., *supra* note 1 and accompanying text.

150   Buckmaster, Stanley et al. *supra* note 5 and accompanying text.

The decision of the case was concluded upon a few main arguments. Firstly, Lord Atkin established a principle based on biblical principles, that people should take care to not harm their neighbours. The term neighbour was then extensively defined, drawing context from several other cases such as *Heaven v. Pender*. In short, not only is a person responsible for not endangering someone in physical proximity to them, but that proximity can extend to anyone who can be directly affected by one's actions, such that that person ought to be kept in mind when performing the action that might affect them.[151] In this example, a manufacturer of ginger beer would certainly consider the drinker of that ginger beer to be their neighbour, given that the purpose of the bottle is to eventually be bought and drunk by the consumer.

Secondly, the court established that any manufacturer has a duty of care towards their consumers and that negligence in itself is a tort— there is no contractual relationship that must be established before this to render the manufacturer, seller, or business liable for any damages they cause.[152]

An ironic note after the fact is that the allegations made by Ms. Donoghue were merely assumed to be true, as there were no investigations made into her claim. Nevertheless, the case certainly brought to light some important questions about common law, such as the question of who a neighbour is.[153]

As the most significant conclusion of this landmark case, the neighbour principle of negligence was established by Lord Atkin. In short, the neighbour principle states that amongst other duties of care, individuals owe a duty of care to take reasonable action that prevents any harm from coming to their neighbours. In this case, a neighbour is defined as anyone who is sufficiently and directly affected enough that one ought to have had this neighbour and the effect they would have on them in mind when acting on the question.[154] In the instance of *Stevenson v. Donoghue,* Dono-

---

151   *Ibid.*

152   *All Answers Ltd., supra* note 1.

153   *Ibid.*

154   Oxford University Press, "Neighbour Principle" (2023) online:

ghue was able to be considered Stevenson's neighbour, as a beer company clearly ought to have the drinker of the bottle and their wellbeing in mind when manufacturing the bottle regardless of whether there was ever a formal contractual relationship established.

Implications of the Landmark Case

Though this case happened on the other side of the world a little less than a century prior, the landmark case of *Donoghue v. Stevenson* introduced the neighbour principle which is used as the basis for many common law cases today across the world. In addition to the manufacturing example that can be seen in the case of *Stevenson v. Donoghue*, this principle can also reasonably be applied to relationships including but not limited to employment relationships, distributing, serving, selling, or other professional relationships.

One example of its extended application is in the field of medicine. When there is a case of medical negligence, even if the medical practitioner was not intentionally attempting to harm the patient, they are still held liable if a couple of conditions are met. Firstly, the fault must be of the healthcare provider(s), hospital, or medical institution. Furthermore, the person must be established to be owed a duty of care, and that duty of care must be breached. Finally, there must be some sort of legally recognized harm that resulted from the negligence of the healthcare provider.[155]

Another sector in which the neighbour principle applies directly in the workplace. Although in most cases there is a clear contractual responsibility that the employer should keep a safe working environment and provide proper training to employees to ensure

---

Oxford Reference <https://www.oxfordreference.com/display/10.1093/oi/authority.20110803100227619;jsessionid=DEB121E00FBBB-B89818A9A87E092805D>.

155   Daniele Bryden & Ian Storey, "Duty of care and medical negligence" (19 June 2011) online: *Oxford University Press* <https://academic.oup.com/bjaed/article/11/4/124/266921>.

there are no safety hazards, the neighbour principle also extends to other parties that may be present in the workplace such as visitors. Regardless of a contractual relationship, a supervisor or employer should always take reasonable efforts to ensure that the environment is free of physical hazards, unsafe working culture, a discriminatory environment, and even the risk of infectious hazards such as COVID-19.[156] These fall under a duty of care to any person they might reasonably expect to enter their workplace.

Transportation is another good example of where the neighbour principle might apply. As a driver, one should immediately keep in mind any passengers as well as the vehicles and pedestrians surrounding them. Furthermore, any merchandise that is being transported should be handled with care, as there are most definitely other parties that would be relying on the safe shipment of those goods. Drivers, conductors, pilots and the like should make reasonable efforts to ensure that their vehicle and the handling of that vehicle does not pose a threat or liability to any of their aforementioned neighbours. These efforts may include regular inspections, proper training, and following any traffic laws.

Lastly, educators also owe a duty of care to their students and other neighbours, such as guest speakers and teaching assistants. This includes ensuring that the content is taught responsibly, ensuring that there is adequate supervision, that no unsafe practices are happening in the classroom, and that all concerns including bullying, discrimination, and harassment are dealt with in a timely and sufficient manner.[157]

---

156   Lisbeth Claus & Yvonne Kallane, "Editorial: Duty of care obligations of employers to protect the health, safety, security and well-being of employees" (October 2015) online: *ResearchGate* <https://www.researchgate.net/publication/305592148_Editorial_Duty_of_care_obligations_of_employers_to_protect_the_health_safety_security_and_well-being_of_employees>.

157   Citizens Information, "Teachers Duty of Care" (20 May 2022) online: *Citizens' Information* <https://www.citizensinformation.ie/en/education/primary_and_post_primary_education/teachers_and_schools/teachers_duty_of_care.html>.

The global influence of Stevenson v. Donoghue

Although *Stevenson v. Donoghue* was a common law landmark case in Scotland, the decision and deliberation made by Lord Atkin received a remarkable amount of attention from legal systems across the globe that took inspiration from the case. Many countries sought to amend or add their common laws on negligence based on the outcomes of this case, with notable examples being the United Kingdom, Canada, Australia, and even surprisingly the United States, which does not rely on the same system of common law. Many other countries across the world have also drawn influence from this case but are not mentioned in this chapter. Later chapters will discuss extensively the case's influence in Australia and Europe.

In Canada, several common law cases have cited *Stevenson v. Donoghue* to determine the duty of care and whether there was negligence. Furthermore, the Canadian judicial system built off of the landmark case to further develop Canadian common law and the process of determining duty of care by citing cases that used the neighbour principle. The most prominent example of this is the case of *Anns v. Merton London Borough Council*— a case from 1977 in the United Kingdom that constructed the two-stage test or the *Anns* test based on the neighbour principle to determine whether there was a duty of care in a scenario.[158] In *Anns v. Merton London Borough Council*, the town's local council approved the construction of a group of residential buildings. During the time of construction, the local council had the legal authority to inspect the construction site and was to be given notice when construction commenced, as well as when the foundation had been laid. Though the local council was allowed to inspect the foundation and order any corrections to them as they saw fit, they were not obligated to do so.[159]

In the case of these maisonettes, the finished foundation was only 2 feet and 6 inches as opposed to the 3 feet or deeper foundations

158   United Kingdom House of Lords, "Anns v Merton London Borough Council" (12 May 1977) online: *Casemine* <https://www.casemine.com/judgement/uk/5a8ff8ca60d03e7f57ecd7a9#>.

159   *Ibid.*

detailed in the original plan. This was likely the reason why, eight years later, the building began to show cracks, slanting, and other defects that caused it to be unsafe for residents to continue living there.[160] Taking legal action, the residents of the building complained about this case of negligence but were initially turned down because the legal action happened too late, given that the first lease contract for the building was signed six years ago. However, they were eventually able to appeal because legal action was taken promptly concerning when the damage ought to have been discovered. In the decision for this case, Lord Wilberforce cited *Stevenson v. Donoghue* to eventually rule in favour of the plaintiffs.[161] In his reasoning, he used a two-step process—firstly using Lord Atkin's neighbour principle, searching for aggravating factors that establish that the council had a duty of care to discover the defect and prevent harm from coming to the tenants. Next, they searched for mitigating factors that suggest that the council did not owe a duty of care to the tenants. In this case, the main potential mitigating factor was the question of whether a statute of limitation applied, meaning whether enough time had passed between when legal action should have first been taken versus when it was taken. Lord Wilberforce recognized that given that there was a bylaw in place that required the builder to notify the council before concealing it with the rest of the building and that the council did not make efforts to exercise that right, there was a degree of negligence.[162] Furthermore, the court decided that the claim was not statute-barred. Canadian common law has cited the Anns test in many common law cases since then but was eventually overturned.[163]

In the United States, *Stevenson v. Donoghue* has been commonly cited as persuasive authority to determine liability in the case of negligence. A notable example of this is the case of *Henningsen v. Bloomfield Motors Inc.* in 1960, which was held in the New Jersey Supreme Court. In this case, the plaintiff had purchased

160   *Ibid.*

161   *Ibid.*

162   Blom, Joost. "Do We Really Need the Anns Test for Duty of Care in Negligence?", (2016), online: *CanLII* <https://canlii.ca/t/6t1>.

163   *Ibid.*

a car from Bloomfield Motors Inc. that contained a defect in the steering system.[164] This defect caused Henningsen to lose control of the vehicle on the road and sustain injuries. In court, it was determined that the principle of duty of care in negligence was applicable as it had been used prevalently in US law before this. Application of the principle was done by citing *Stevenson v. Donoghue.*[165]

Reflections and Conclusion

The case of *Stevenson v Donoghue* is regarded by many as having one of the greatest legacies in the world of common law, arguing that its influence is vast and can be commonly seen even in subtle amounts. However, others argue that the nature of common law and its precedents are such that the outcome and impact of this case are not as straightforward as one might expect, with certain drivers such as circumstance, social factors, and the unique characteristics of each notable person having just as equal of a hand in shaping the fate of common law as what one might call logical deliberation. For example, Allan Hutchinson from Osgoode Hall Law School questions, what would the law surrounding negligence look like if Donoghue did not accompany her friend to the cafe on that day? Or perhaps, what if the Lord giving the judgment was not Lord Atkin, but some other judge?[166] Since common law is so dependent on the unfolding of real events rather than the theoretical deliberation of a systematic law, the question of "what if" lingers.

---

164   CaseBriefs. "Henningsen v. Bloomfield Motors, Inc", (2021), online: *CaseBriefs* <https://www.casebriefs.com/blog/law/contracts/contracts-keyed-to-farnsworth/policing-the-bargain/henningsen-v-bloomfield-motors-inc-2/>.

165   *Ibid.*

166   Allan Hutchinson, "Some 'What If' Thoughts: Notes on Donoghue v Stevenson" (2014) online: *Osgoode Hall Law Journal* <https://digitalcommons.osgoode.yorku.ca/cgi/viewcontent.cgi?referer=&httpsredir=1&article=2736&context=ohlj>.

It is certainly possible that even if the events of *Stevenson v. Donoghue* had been interrupted, perhaps Ms. Donoghue or another individual would have eventually set common law down the same course it is on today, at a different time and place. Furthermore, Hutchinson argues that the reason the Paisley Snail case received so much traction from Lord Atkin's decision is largely due to the socio-political appeal and intellectual acceptability.[167] Therefore, it could be suggested that if the case had not turned out the way it did, the neighbour principle or a principle similar to it would have eventually been derived from some other case in the common law.

---

167   *Ibid.*

Chapter 8: *Donoghue v. Stevenson*, Temporal Development

David Supina

What might be gained from an examination of *Donoghue v. Stevenson* through a philosophical examination? Such an examination may assess the robustness of the principles involved. The very operations of law are an appeal to a hierarchy of principles, even if it might be seen with some scepticism: "It is not easy to explain why a legal system which in its law of real property displays some of the most intricate concepts ever conceived in the human mind, should show itself so hostile to speculative analysis. But so it is: warnings against too ready a reliance on what is called "philosophy" or "logic" are common enough in the books; most lawyers have equated "philosophy" to metaphysics. Fortunately, it has been recently been realised that one may be a philosopher without being committed to the view that there exist transcendental concepts of universal validity which if one were only clever enough to discover their true essence, provide a criterion for judging the rightness of all conduct".[168] However, all reasoning operates from principles, even if it is only the principle of the coherence of reasoning. One can question the premises of

168   Heuston, R. F. V. "Donoghue v. Stevenson in Retrospect." The Modern Law Review, vol. 20, no. 1, Jan. 1957, pp. 1–24. EBSCOhost, discovery.ebsco.com/linkprocessor/plink?id=b621faa6-346b-3005-89fb-1e3a3b8800a1 [*Heuston*].

a syllogism all one wants, but one cannot make valid deductions until they are used. As such, a grounding in metaphysics that is coherent with the legal principles intended to be upheld would help. But metaphysics has wide-ranging applications, and people are not perfectly reasoned out systems of belief. It is far too big a project to try to lay out a full system of belief from metaphysical principles to specific applications of the law, but we can begin somewhere and reason from one or more principles, and care for neighbours via the neighbour principle or duty of care, is a place to start. For the sake of simplicity, the parties represented in the case *Donoghue v. Stevenson* are referred to by their names "Donoghue" and "Stevenson".

Is there a moral duty?

The principle of the duty of care does engender serious questions about the extent to which legal limitations can be applied to holding parties legally responsible when there is no explicit contractual relationship between parties. Some sort of basis must be sought for the extent to which moral duties become legal ones. Of course, the simplest approach would be to erase the line altogether and simply assert that if something is a moral duty, it should be a legal one as well. But this does not answer the question, because even assuming a stable basis upon which to determine morally good from morally compromised, there is the question of what just punishment is for every crime. While it is imaginable to have every moral wrongdoing, thus in this theoretical case every crime, carries the same punishment. Such a state seems morally repugnant on the face of it, so it seems obvious to reject it. We must then make a distinction between acts which are punishment enough in themselves, and those that warrant further intervention. Some things can be theoretically more serious moral violations and yet require little legal intervention, such as the harm done by adultery, whereas petty theft may require at least a little punishment. However, this does appeal to our intuitions that there is something of a sense of a sliding scale of moral violations from inconsequential to requiring the most solemn repudiation and punishment. A shade of self-absorption is not the same degree of seriousness as a serial killer, and the exact placement of moral acts along that continuity is certainly worthy of consideration. But we can proceed on to other matters with at least the recognition that there is such a scale, and it isn't one-to-one with the amount of legal intervention required.

The very principle upon which the duty of care rests, the neighbour principle, can be challenged. "the 'neighbour principle' has not merely been over-emphasized, but has been canonised and made the very foundation of the law of negligence. Seldom in the history of the common law has a single statement of a single judge in a single case had such a profound effect on the development of the law."[169] However, it is still probably the consent of most involved that the law should be concerned with justice, and what is justice if not a right action towards others, and others not sorted through arbitrarily? "What kind of morality is this, which makes neighbours out of strangers? Scholars have noted not only the moral foundation of the neighbour principle but also its ambivalent status *as* a principle."[170] If there is a limit to how one ought to act justly, it is limited to those who are likely to be affected by one's actions, which grows increasingly in a globalized world. It would seem arbitrary to limit whether, say, nefarious activities online are not liable to legal responsibility merely because they may not affect one's, physical neighbours.[171] The neighbours of this principle may occasionally be distant, but it is consistent insofar as one is made neighbour by some form of contact, in which a negligent act, or an act of un-neighbourliness if that term is preferred, might take place.

---

169   Smith, J. C., and Peter Burns. "Donoghue v. Stevenson: The Not So Golden Anniversary." The Modern Law Review, vol. 46, no. 2, Mar. 1983, pp. 147–63. EBSCOhost, discovery.ebsco.com/linkprocessor/plink?id=9ade4b83-e3c7-3fc3-a9b4-46a2b14499d3 [*Smith & Burns*].

170   Van Rijswijk, Honni. "Mabel Hannah's Justice: A Contextual Re-Reading of Donoghue v Stevenson." Public Space: The Journal of Law & Social Justice, vol. 5, June 2010, pp. 1–26. EBSCOhost, https://doi-org.ezproxy.aekc.talonline.ca/10.5130/psjlsj.v5i0.1903 [*Van Rijswijk*].

171   *Smith & Burns, supra* note 168.

Considerations of responsibility are the domain of religion as well as the law, and in the Roman Rite Mass, at a section called the Confiteor, the people together say, "I have greatly sinned [...] in what I have done and *in what I have failed to do*".[172] The temptation for the conscience is to bracket out the things that are the result of our inactions, and perhaps there is a parallel legal temptation to give a pass to harm due to inaction. Had the manufacturer intentionally put a snail in the bottle, it seems that there would have been a clearer basis for the case. But if there is a moral basis for violations being based on inaction, can there not be a legal one as well? It suggests at least a basis for negligence being a potential violation of expected public conduct. Whether Stevenson, quite apart from any legal rulings, is morally responsible comes down to whether or not he could have reasonably been expected to keep snails out of his bottles. Were there procedures he could have implemented that would have kept the bottles clean had he been concerned about the general safety of what he was selling?

There is another aspect in moving from the realm of religion, where our conscience might accuse us, to the realm of civil law, which is that in a religious context, we might feel compelled to take actions to reconcile our negligence with the just God we purport to serve, and maybe do so privately through prayer or a Sacrament, and perhaps there might even be a seeking of reconciliation with the offended party, but for restitution in civil law, much more may be demanded.[173] There may be restitution to be done in the form of financial compensation, and there may be punishment attached that is much more severe than any sort of penance that may flow from religious duty. There is also a fundamental difference. In a religious response to a negligent act, there may be just one or several parties involved. In instances where a religious minister and an offended person are involved, for example, case details may not be publicly available. To be publicly taken through the courts is like airing one's dirty laundry, and may be analogous to legal self-penance.

---

172   *Van Rijswijk, supra* note 169.

173   *Ibid.*

Perhaps there should be some reluctance to make everything ac-
knowledged as wrongdoing, even in theory, be a matter brought
before the courts. But then, what are the criteria for sorting
through what can be a matter of private conscience, and what can
rise to the level of needing public judgment and punishment? One
criterion that springs to mind is the severity of the impugned act.
If a child steals money from their parents, it seems unnecessary
to put them on trial for that. If someone steals twenty million
dollars from their company, however, then it does seem to be
more appropriately resolved before the courts since the crime's
scope is more serious. Yet, there is another factor to consider.
Suppose a child steals $1000 from their relatively poor parents
after becoming an adult. The child's adulthood may exacerbate
the action's severity, but should the adult child be brought to
trial? Not necessarily. If the adult child is remorseful and willing
to make restitution, and reconciliation between family members
appears possible, then the incident may not need to escalate into
public prosecution. But if the adult child is obstinate, refuses to
make restitution, or reconciles with their parents, society may be
justified to pursue legal action. Government intervention would
be valid even if the parents hope to eventually reconcile with
their child or if the child eventually becomes remorseful. Even
in the case of the twenty million dollars, is it possible that if the
company could recover most or all of the money, they could
then simply fire the wrongdoing employee but press no further
charges? Perhaps from the company's perspective, yes. However,
societal norms regarding expected conduct would not allow such
actions to remain unpunished. There are concerns with letting
someone that committed such a serious crime "walk-off" without punishment since they may recidivate or be hired by another
future company with the worker's behavioural risks unbeknownst
to them.

Implications

What's interesting about *Donoghue v. Stevenson* is that in terms
of the ability to mediate, while the previous examples were those
with people who had an established relationship through which

the problem could potentially be sorted without the use of courts, Donoghue and Stevenson were very distantly connected. Re-consider the question, "Who is my neighbour". Stevenson sold a product to a café that was bought by Donoghue's friend and then drank by Donoghue. The only real link between them was the impersonal link of commerce.[174] It seems unlikely that such a relationship, as tenuous as it is, could be settled easily between the two. Perhaps Donoghue could write a letter of complaint, but without the clear legal precedent of duty towards a person who was not legally a customer of his product, why would Stevenson be moved to compensate her? However, if we operate from a principle that by having any sort of contact at all, there is a sort of neighbour relationship, then there is a reasonable and coherent principle upon which to operate. The downside is the net is cast wide, especially in our globally connected world. But then, maybe that is just the reality of the world in which we live.

The other thing to consider then is if this is serious enough to warrant legal recourse, and that's not as simple as it first may seem. The consequence on the person of Mrs. Donoghue was serious, yes, but it is possible to have a serious consequence for a perfectly innocent action.[175] For example, if someone goes to a restaurant and orders a meal but forgets to mention their allergy to an ingredient that is in the food, then the chef should not be responsible for normal preparations of the food which may then result in the person eating it becoming hospitalised. The chef is not responsible because they do not have any reasonable way of being aware of the person's circumstances. Just because an action (cooking with an allergen) has a bad consequence (hospitalisation) does not automatically mean that the person who caused the bad thing to happen is culpable for their action.

So, is keeping snails (and other small creatures) out of bottles a reasonable ask, to the point that failing to do so should be met with legal punishment? Consider the question of whether there was wrongdoing. Before we ask the question of whether it was wrongdoing that ought to be punished legally, the perspective

174   *Heuston, supra* note 167.

175   *Ibid.*

of the issue should be whether Stevenson could have reasonably done otherwise.[176] In other words, was there a moral duty towards taking appropriate care of his product to keep it safe from contaminants that he did not take? This is where the transition from the realm of religion, conscience and private conviction becomes tricky. The only absolute arbiter of whether he was neglectful in snail avoidance is Stevenson's conscience if he knew he could have done more to keep his bottles from contaminants but did not bother, or God, who is likely going to be unavailable for comment. How can someone be held publicly responsible? Well, by the ruling, it seems that the judgment was that by the mere presence of a snail, there was evidence of a dereliction of duty.

The problem seems to be that no matter the amount of effort to prevent contamination from happening, there is always going to be a chance that it does. Suppose that Stevenson set up the world's greatest anti-snail bottling process after losing his case—he may have been more efficient at keeping snails out of his bottles than any of his contemporary competitors. But, if just one single snail snuck through, whereas due to better luck, his more lackadaisical competitors managed to stay snail free, who is going to get punished for the next snail in a bottle incident? Especially if he's already been caught once with this problem, Stevenson is likely going to be held liable for what amounts to enormously bad luck. This means that to judge these things correctly, there needs to be a consideration for the possibility that the particular case may be a statistical anomaly from a company or person that is otherwise taking due care. There does seem to be a problem with judging there to be neglect by sheer virtue of there being a defect because occasionally highly statistically unlikely things do occur.

Reasonable care

So, what is the principle upon which a reasonable amount of care can be judged to either have been exercised or not exercised?

---

176   *Van Rijswijk, supra* note 169.

For a precaution to be expected, the possible damage must be foreseeable, it must be either avoidable or at least possible to minimize through taking some sort of intervention, and it must be logistically possible to carry out.[177]

The ability for possible harm to be foreseen would potentially change over time. The possibility of contaminants in opaque glass bottles may demand more precautions as it becomes clear that people are having, say, snails or mice sneak into the bottles. But is that culpability merely reduced or is it removed altogether if a particular hazard occurs for the first time? Well, it would depend on whether it could have been anticipated as a possible source of harm beforehand.[178] If it is the first time anything of the sort has occurred, it may be reasonable to say that there was a lack of foreseeability of the consequences, which may make it fair to absolve a party of liability. However, just because something hasn't happened yet doesn't mean that a consequence is not foreseeable. The NHL has yet to ban fighting from the game, but just because nobody has died from taking part in a fight on NHL ice, does that mean it's not foreseeable? The potential harm of that continued practice is quite apparent.

There also needs to be some sort of effective intervention. Perhaps with all the safe handling of a glass bottle, a small percentage cracks, and is therefore hazardous to handle. There might be nothing more that can be done in the transportation process to keep these bottles from very occasionally cracking, and perhaps even a percentage of those are going to get as far as being sold to a customer. If everything is already being done to keep them from cracking, it would be unreasonable to expect anything more. Tied to this condition is whether any changes to reduce potential harm are logistically possible. Instructing delivery people to handle it in a maximally safe way is one thing, but maybe what it would take to keep them all from cracking is to cut down each shipment per truck in half and then spend labour-intensive time individually wrapping every bottle in cloth. But such action may result in costs doubling or tripling costs, which may mean that the prof-

---

177   *Heuston, supra* note 167.
178   *Ibid.*

itability of the entire enterprise may be compromised by these procedures to ensure that no cracked bottles are delivered. Is this logistically possible then? Not for a for-profit company, no.

But is the mere inability to make a profit enough to excuse someone from making things entirely safe? The reality Is that If we intended to build a society where we cast aside any prioritizing of profit in exchange for an extreme emphasis on safety, we could do so. But for as popular as it is to decry profit or even basic economics, but without an extensive defence of some form of capitalism, it is worth remarking that it is not a given that we should simply not value the ability to allow people to function in an economic system that allows them to find profitable ways to operate, without smothering it entirely for the sake of a single-minded focus on safety.[179] After all, it is not merely that we want to live long and healthy lives, we also want the quality of that life to be good, and that would be much more difficult if every venture in which we could invent for ourselves a livelihood, in the form of a small business or similar, was choked to the point of inaction by requiring strict and maximal safety requirements at every turn.

If there is something to be called for, it's that profitability and safety are both good ends, if we can make room for both in our metaphysics, but only to a certain point.[180] Profitability is a vice insofar as it trods on safety and other human values in its pursuit, and safety is a vice when to avoid relatively minor harm whole industries are shut down for what is now an impossibility of making any sort of profit. The governing idea I would suggest to which judgments must be submitted is the common good, which may be instinctively known by anyone who is not overly partisan. Partiality to the common good is a part of human psychology (even spirituality), it is the part of ourselves that baulks when a company pursues profit to the extent of causing public endangerment or pauses at the inability of a small business to navigate unnecessarily complex safety regulations (bureaucratic red tape existing for the sake of red tape), is exactly the part that should be making the judgment of when a given line is crossed.

---

179   *Smith & Burns, supra* note 168.
180   *Ibid.*

So as much as we circle around and back, we find ourselves irreducibly at the mercy of human judgment. This is not to say that said judgment must be neutral, but it should aspire to impartiality. Impartiality is a lower, and much more humanly attainable standard than neutrality. It is enough to make a distinctly human judgement, as to whether a particular case is liable due to a general duty of care, that one is not overly attached to either party or their argument, *a priori*.[181] To be neutral demands far more, and far too much from a human being, because it would demand that we judge with no preconceptions, no tendencies, no guiding principles. But to think humanly is precisely to operate with such factors, and it is difficult, perhaps impossible, to imagine a human mind that is truly neutral. The neutral human mind is the one absent of all humanity. So, when we think of the examples discussed, is it reasonable to hold Stevenson responsible for his snail? From my preconceptions, tendencies and guiding principles, I would say yes, but even in the case itself, the decision was split 3-2.[182] Can we go forward with only three out of five deciding that decision should be one way rather than the other?

To some extent, we have made peace with a degree of dissent in any country that operates as a democracy. As much as this author may be partial to the idea of monarchies, we have learned to live with systems in which our governments are run by people who were chosen by a slim majority, or even a little less than that in the case of the Canadian Federal government. The nature of the judgments we make is that they can be, and usually are, questioned. So, we do have to go forward knowing that the human process of making judgments as to whether a duty of care has been violated, or whether it is by principle outside the realm of what can be reasonably asserted to be duty, is intrinsically fuzzy.

---

181   *Van Rijswijk, supra* note 169.

182   Armitage, Chris. "Lord Atkin, the Snail and the Foreigner: Loving the Neighbour and Oppressing the Alien." Law & Humanities, vol. 16, no. 1, June 2022, pp. 123–44. EBSCOhost, https://doi-org. ezproxy.aekc.talonline.ca/10.1080/17521483.2022.2073524.

Artificial Intelligence

But what about the case of artificial intelligence? Surely, an AI could make judgments that are unencumbered by human preconceptions. The problem is that the total absence of all preconceptions is just as bad or worse than having a bunch of bad ones. There have been several instances of AI chat systems exhibiting racist behaviour because they indiscriminately learned it from human behaviour.[183] The preconception that human life is intrinsically valuable is not something an AI knows natively, and even if we want a particular AI to have that quality, we are at the mercy of its programmers as to how well they can abstract the concept of the dignity of human life into something that translates into machine code, into binary, essentially. What number is human dignity? If such a question seems strange, then that suggests an appreciation of how difficult it is to translate distinctly human qualities into artificial intelligence. AI, as it currently exists, is a series of processes, that just happen to be performed at incredible speed. But there is a fundamental difference between a process and an agent.[184] An agent uses processes, a process is performed, but even recursively, it does not "use" itself in the same way an agent may use such a process, because an agent has an aim, whereas a process can only simulate an aim, which has to be fed to it by an agent, namely its programmer. Whether agency could become an emergent element of the processes used to build AI remains to be seen, but given what a black box consciousness is, it seems a leap to presume that merely faster computational power will lead to artificial consciousness.

---

183   Buranyi, Stephen. "Rise of the Racist Robots--how AI Is Learning All of Our Worst Impulses." *The Guardian*, 8 Aug. 2017, www.theguardian.com/inequality/2017/aug/08/rise-of-the-racist-robots-how-ai-is-learning-all-our-worst-impulses. Accessed 31 Mar. 2023.

184   *Ibid.*

Conclusion

Perhaps there is something to be said that perhaps as much as humans like simplicity, there is a degree of complexity that emerges at one end or the other. There can either be simple principles, like the neighbour principle that lead to a great deal of complexity in terms of application, or there can be a complex system of application, applying many contingencies and provisions so that the process of judgement is little more than following a flow chart. Comparatively speaking, it seems better to have simple principles as long as they are well-founded. This is because simple principles allow for interesting and creative applications of those same principles and that may lead to more room for justice than trying to create laws for all conceivable circumstances. The latter would inevitably result in some circumstance that is unaccounted for. Putting aside the hope for perfection in the pursuit of what is for the good is always a deeply human and reasonable move.

Chapter 9: The Influence of *Donoghue v. Stevenson* in Australia

Rameen Tanveer

Law is a fascinating field that has a significant impact on society. It shapes the way we interact with each other and provides a framework for resolving conflicts. In Australia, the legal system has evolved, with significant cases helping to shape the way we think about justice and the law. One such case is *Donoghue v. Stevenson*, a landmark case that has had a profound impact on the law in Australia and around the world.

Donoghue v. Stevenson is a prime example of a landmark case that has had a significant impact on the law. It has established important legal principles that have been used to determine liability in cases of negligence, and its influence can be seen in the way that the law has developed in Australia and around the world. By examining the case and its implications, we can gain a better understanding of the role that landmark cases play in shaping the law and the impact they can have on society as a whole.

In this chapter, we will explore the influence of *Donoghue v. Stevenson* in Australia. Specifically, an overview of the case in Australian law, the legal principles established in *Donoghue v. Stevenson* and how they have been applied in subsequent cases. As well as, exploring some of the key debates and controversies that have arisen in the wake of this influential case.

Overview

In Australian law, *Donoghue v. Stevenson* is a landmark case that
has had significant implications on the legal system. The impact
of the *Donoghue v. Stevenson* case was felt not only in the UK
but also in Commonwealth countries like Australia. One of the
key concepts established by the case is the duty of care owed
by manufacturers to consumers. Duty of care is a legal obligation imposed on an individual or organization to act reasonably
and prudently to avoid causing harm to others. In *Donoghue v.
Stevenson*, the court held that a manufacturer owes a duty of care
to consumers who use their products, even in the absence of a
direct contractual relationship. This duty extends to ensuring that
the products produced are safe and free from defects. The case
has been considered a cornerstone of tort law in Australia, and it
has affected the evolution of negligence law in the nation.[185] The
case's judgment has been cited in many Australian court cases,
and the concepts established by the case are commonly used by
courts when deciding negligence claims. Additionally, the case
has influenced Australian consumer protection legislation. The
principles established in the case have been integrated into other
consumer protection acts, notably the Australian Consumer Law,
which seeks to protect consumers against dangerous products and
misleading company practices.

Donoghue v. Stevenson is one of the most famous and significant
tort law decisions in history. The case is widely recognized as a
landmark case in Australian tort law, and it has had a substantial
influence on the development of tort law in Australia. The case
exemplifies the negligence concept, which has evolved to play a
critical role in Australian tort law.

Mrs. Donoghue visited a café in Paisley, Scotland, in 1932, when
a friend bought her a bottle of ginger beer. Mrs. Donoghue drank
some of the beer, and when her friend finished the bottle, she

185   David F Jackson, "The Australian Judicial System: Judicial
Power of the Commonwealth" (8 March 2021) online: *HeinOnline*
<https://heinonline.org/HOL/LandingPage?handle=hein.journals%2Fsw
ales24&div=67&id=&page=>.

discovered the remains of a decomposed snail in her glass. Mrs. Donoghue became unwell after drinking the beer, suffering from shock and gastroenteritis. She subsequently sued Mr. Stevenson, the ginger beer's producer, for monetary damages, saying that he owed her a duty of care, which he broke by allowing the snail to remain present in the bottle.

The case went to court, where it was argued that Mr. Stevenson, as the manufacturer of the ginger beer, had a duty of care to ensure that the drink was safe to consume. The court found in favour of Mrs. Donoghue, holding that Mr. Stevenson had a duty of care to ensure that his products were safe and that he had breached this duty by allowing the snail to be present in the bottle. This decision established the principle of negligence, which holds that a person who owes a duty of care to another can be held liable for damages if that duty is breached. The matter was heard in court, where it was claimed that Mr. Stevenson, as the maker of the ginger beer, owed a duty of care to guarantee that the drink was safe to drink. The court ruled in favour of Mrs. Donoghue, stating that Mr. Stevenson owed Mrs. Donoghue a duty of care to ensure the safety of his products and that he broke that obligation by permitting the snail to be present in the bottle. This case established the negligence concept, which states that a person who owes another a duty of care can be held accountable for damages if that obligation is broken.[186]

In the end, *Donoghue v. Stevenson* is still recognised as a landmark case and is an important case that has had a significant impact on the development of tort law in Australia. Since its ruling, the case has been cited in other judgments, and its principles have been extended to address a wide variety of scenarios. The case has also had a considerable influence on the creation of consumer protection laws, which have been put in place to hold manufacturers accountable for the safety of their products.

---

186   D N MacCormick, "Formal justice and the form of legal arguments - JSTOR" (1976) online: *JSTOR* <https://www.jstor.org/stable/44084511>.

Impact of Donoghue v. Stevenson in Australia

Donoghue v. Stevenson was a significant case that transformed the legal concepts of negligence and duty of care. This case established the standard for determining duty of care in negligence claims in Australian and international courts.

The concepts established in *Donoghue v. Stevenson* have been applied in several instances in Australia, influencing the evolution of tort law. *Grant v. Australian Knitting Mills Ltd*, which contained a similar set of circumstances, was one of the most significant cases that relied on *Donoghue v. Stevenson*.

In this case, the plaintiff, Grant, developed an itching rash after wearing an undergarment made by Australian Knitting Mills Ltd. Grant sued the firm claiming that the undergarment was faulty and caused his injuries. The Privy Council settled the issue, ruling that the firm was accountable for Grant's harm. The court reasoned that the corporation owed consumers a duty of care by permitting defective underwear to be marketed. It was also determined that the fault caused Grant's injuries and that he was entitled to compensation as a result.[187]

Grant v. Australian Knitting Mills Ltd is, in many aspects, an extension of the concepts outlined in *Donoghue v. Stevenson*. Both judgements included negligence lawsuits against manufacturers, and both established that manufacturers had a duty of care to customers to guarantee the safety of their products. *Grant v. Australian Knitting Mills Ltd.* also served to define the scope of this duty of care, finding that it applies not just to bodily damage but also to economic loss.

The connection between *Donoghue v. Stevenson* and *Grant v. Australian Knitting Mills Ltd* emphasizes the significance of major decisions in influencing the law. *Donoghue v. Stevenson* established a broad negligence concept that has been used in numerous instances, whereas *Grant v. Australian Knitting Mills Ltd* served to define and refine the reach of this principle in the context of

---

187   W G Friedmann, "Social Insurance and the Principles of Tort Liability" (1949) online: *JSTOR* <*https://about.jstor.org/oa-and-free/*>.

product liability. Together, these cases have had a significant influence on the evolution of tort law in Australia and across the world, and they are still cited and relied on by courts today.

Another important case that was influenced by *Donoghue v. Stevenson* was *Rogers v. Whitaker.* The case involved a patient, Mrs. Rogers, who received an eye procedure done by Dr. Whitaker. Mrs. Rogers told Dr. Whitaker that she was particularly worried about the possibility of retinal detachment since she only had sight in one eye. Despite this, Dr. Whitaker neglected to inform Mrs. Rogers about the higher risk of retinal detachment connected with the treatment, and the operation resulted in retinal detachment, rendering Mrs. Rogers entirely blind.[188]

The ruling in *Rogers v. Whitaker* is very similar to *Donoghue v. Stevenson*. Both instances include a professional's duty of care to their client, as well as the necessity to demonstrate that duty and breach of that duty to find responsibility. The court stressed the significance of the concept of informed consent in *Rogers v. Whitaker*, which compels doctors to communicate any relevant risks connected with surgery to their patients. This approach extends the negligence principle established in *Donoghue v. Stevenson* to circumstances involving medical practitioners. The case established that a doctor's duty of care includes a positive requirement to warn patients of any serious dangers involved with a medical operation, regardless of whether the patient expressly requests it.[189] This idea has been utilized in several cases, resulting in the increased patient protection and a higher level of care among medical practitioners.

---

188   Don Chalmers & Robert Schwartz, "Rogers v. Whitaker and informed consent in Australia: a fair dinkum duty of disclosure" (1993) online: *Oxford Academic* <https://academic.oup.com/medlaw/article-abstract/1/2/139/1092477?redirectedFrom=PDF&casa_token=7znpmzOXI4IAAAAA%3Ad0sUXKyqsTn6DWZJOb303mpmWe-QrUkDWhMhaHHDX0QCwrItDh5M09wCJJUVze1-uqqcM39tXwjYzg>.

189   The Hon. Justice Susan Kiefel, "Developments in the Law Relating to Medical Negligence in the Last 30 Years" (8 March 2021) online: *HeinOnline* <https://heinonline.org/HOL/LandingPage?handle=hein.journals%2Fitbla19&div=4&id=&page=>.

After the ruling of the *Donoghue v. Stevenson* case, Australian law established that manufacturers have a duty of care to consumers, which means they must ensure that their products are safe and do not pose a risk of harm to consumers. This principle has since been incorporated into various consumer protection statutes in Australia, including *Australian Consumer Law* Act. For example, section 138 of the *Australian Consumer Law* states that a manufacturer must not supply goods that are not of acceptable quality, including goods that are unsafe or that do not meet any express warranties or guarantees.[190] This provision reflects the principle established in *Donoghue v. Stevenson* that manufacturers owe a duty of care to consumers and must take reasonable steps to ensure that their products are safe. Another example is found in section 236 of the Australian Consumer Law, which provides for remedies when goods are not of acceptable quality or do not meet other consumer guarantees.[191] This section allows consumers to seek compensation for damages or to seek a replacement or refund when goods do not meet acceptable standards, including safety requirements.

Donoghue v Stevenson and Product Liability

The landmark case of *Donoghue v Stevenson* significantly impacted the development of product liability law in Australia, as well as other common law jurisdictions. This case established the foundation of modern tort law by giving rise to the "neighbour principle", which imposes a duty of care on manufacturers to avoid causing harm to their consumers.[192] The ruling in this case by the House of Lords marked a radical departure from the exist-

---

190   The Australian Consumer Law, "The Australian Consumer Law" (2011) online: *Australian Consumer Law* <https://consumer.gov. au/australian-consumer-law/legislation>.

191   *Ibid* at s 236.

192   J C Smith and Peter Burns, "Economic action and social structure: The problem of embeddedness," (1983), online: *JSTOR* <https://www.jstor.org/stable/pdf/2780199.pdf?casa_token=GnmQY-WZ0tYkAAAAA:-acguEoEtP0oiToXTR5vQgCwIs4BR3xHT0e-ZaF6rsldg2NmFk91bEUSoYYcwK72jYd14ogyrnXo96AduOaEnnPz-j5nvswm1XASNznuD6zE251Tu0gGE>.

ing legal principles, as it rejected the privity of contract doctrine that had previously governed the relationship between consumers and manufacturers.

The significance of *Donoghue v Stevenson* in product liability law in Australia can be attributed to the creation of the duty of care owed by manufacturers to consumers, regardless of the absence of a direct contractual relationship. This duty extends to ensuring that the products they produce are safe and free from defects. The case has had a profound influence on Australian law, with the High Court of Australia expressly endorsing the decision and the "neighbour principle" in the case of *Grant v. Australian Knitting Mills Ltd*.[193] Since then, Australian courts have relied on the *Donoghue v Stevenson* decision to develop a comprehensive body of product liability law.

In Australia, the application of the principle established in *Donoghue v. Stevenson* has been evident in numerous cases involving product liability. One such case is *Australian Knitting Mills Ltd v. Grant*, in which the High Court applied the neighbour principle to hold a manufacturer liable for injuries caused by defective clothing.[194] Over time, the principles established in Donoghue v Stevenson have also been codified into Australian legislation. The introduction of the *Australian Consumer Law* (ACL), specifically in Part 3-5 - Liability of Manufacturers for Goods with Safety Defects, reflects the influence of *Donoghue v. Stevenson* on Australia's product liability framework. The ACL imposes strict liability on manufacturers and importers for harm caused by defective goods, further emphasizing the responsibility of these parties to ensure the safety of their products for consumers.

The impact of *Donoghue v. Stevenson* has also been felt in other areas of tort law. For example, the case has influenced the development of the law of negligence relating to services, as seen in cases such as *Hedley Byrne & Co Ltd v. Heller & Partners Ltd*, where the House of Lords extended the duty of care to negligent

---

193   Martin Davies, "Reading Cases" (1987) online: *JSTOR* <https://www.jstor.org/stable/1096339>>.

194   *Ibid* at 410.

misstatements causing economic loss.[195] In Australia, the High Court has also recognized a duty of care in cases of negligent advice, as demonstrated by the landmark decision in Shaddock v Parramatta City Council.[196]

Furthermore, the principle of duty of care established in *Donoghue v. Stevenson* has been influential in shaping the law on omissions and third-party liability. In cases such as *Stovin v. Wise* and *Perre v. Apand Pty Ltd*, the courts have grappled with the issue of when a duty of care arises for a defendant's failure to act or for harm caused by the actions of a third party.[197] The neighbour principle has played a crucial role in informing these decisions and guiding the development of the law in these areas.

The legacy of *Donoghue v. Stevenson* also extends to the broader implications of the duty of care for public policy and the regulation of various industries. The case has prompted increased scrutiny of product safety standards and has led to the establishment of various regulatory bodies and the implementation of stricter regulations in areas such as food safety, pharmaceuticals, and consumer products. The impact of the case on public policy has led to a heightened awareness of consumer rights and the importance of ensuring that manufacturers are held accountable for the safety and quality of their products.

To this day, the *Donoghue v. Stevenson* case continues to shape product liability law in Australia. Its establishment of the neighbour principle and the duty of care owed by manufacturers to

---

195   A Honore, "Hedley Byrne & (and) Co., Ltd. v. Heller & (and) Partners, Ltd.," (8 March 2021), online: *HeinOnline* <https://heinonline.org/HOL/LandingPage?handle=hein.journals%2F-sptlns8&div=39&id=&page=>.

196   J Johnson, "Shaddock & Associates Pty Ltd and Another v Parramatta City Council," (1982), online: *Sage Journals* <https://journals.sagepub.com/doi/abs/10.1177/0067205X8201300106>.

197   Jane Convey, "Public or Private? Duty of Care in a Statutory Framework: Stovin v Wise in the House of Lords" (1997), online: *JSTOR* https://www.jstor.org/stable/1097215>.; Joachim Dietrich, "Liability in negligence for pure economic loss: the latest chapter (Perre v Apand Pty Ltd)" (2000) online: *InformIT* <https://www.informit.com/>.

consumers has been instrumental in the development of Australian tort law, as well as the introduction of statutory provisions like the *Australian Consumer Law*. This case has not only transformed the legal landscape in Australia but has also had a lasting impact on the protection of consumer rights and interests concerning product safety.

Criticisms and Limitations of Donoghue v. Stevenson

Despite the transformative impact of *Donoghue v. Stevenson* on the law of negligence in Australia, there have been criticisms and limitations associated with the principle of duty of care and its application. One criticism is the potential ambiguity and subjectivity in determining the scope of the duty of care, which may lead to inconsistent outcomes and uncertainties for both claimants and defendants. Additionally, the broad nature of the principle has raised concerns about excessive litigation and the financial burden on businesses and public authorities.

The principle of duty of care also faces limitations in cases involving economic loss, public authorities, and policy considerations. While some Australian cases have extended the duty of care to cover pure economic loss, such as in *Perre v. Apand Pty Ltd*, establishing a duty of care in this context remains challenging due to concerns about indeterminate liability and the potential for an unmanageable number of claims. For public authorities, courts are often cautious in imposing a duty of care, as it may interfere with the allocation of resources and the decision-making processes of these entities, potentially leading to a detrimental impact on public policy.[198]

In medical negligence cases, the principle of duty of care established in *Donoghue v. Stevenson* has had to be adapted to accommodate the complexities of the doctor-patient relationship and the

---

198   Dale Hutchison, "Relational Economic Loss (or Interference with Contractual Relations): The Last Hurdle" (8 March 2021) online: *HeinOnline* <https://heinonline.org/HOL/LandingPage?handle=hein.journals%2Factj2000&div=11&id=&page=>.

unique challenges of determining liability in a healthcare context. Cases such as *Rogers v. Whitaker* and *Montgomery v Lanarkshire Health Board* have built upon the foundation laid by *Donoghue v Stevenson* but have also demonstrated the need for ongoing refinement and development of the duty of care concept in this area. [199] [200]

To address these criticisms and limitations, several proposals for reform and alternative approaches have been suggested. One proposal is to develop clearer guidelines for determining the scope of the duty of care, providing a more predictable and structured approach for courts to follow. This could include the adoption of a multi-factorial test, such as the one used in the United States under the "foreseeability" test, which evaluates factors like proximity, relationship, and the likelihood of harm.[201]

Another proposal is to introduce statutory provisions that clearly define the scope of liability for public authorities and cases involving economic loss, similar to the *Civil Liability Act* in some Australian states and territories. This approach could provide greater clarity and certainty for both claimants and defendants while ensuring that public policy concerns are adequately addressed.[202]

Finally, alternative approaches to resolving negligence claims,

199   Mark Campbell, "Montgomery v Lanarkshire Health Board" (2015) online: *Sage Journals* <https://journals.sagepub.com/doi/10.1177/1473779515592118>.

200   *Chalmers and Schwartz, supra* note 100.

201   Doug Cassel, "Outlining the case for a common law duty of care of business to exercise human rights due diligence: Business and Human Rights Journal" (21 April 2016) online: *Cambridge Core* <https://www.cambridge.org/core/journals/business-and-human-rights-journal/article/abs/outlining-the-case-for-a-common-law-duty-of-care-of-business-to-exercise-human-rights-due-diligence/0AC3AC3B131615011C802628A1750408>.

202   Hadfield, Gillian. "Legal Barriers to Innovation: The Growing Economic Cost of Professional Control over Corporate Legal Markets", (8 March 2021), online: HeinOnline <https://heinonline.org/HOL/LandingPage?handle=hein.journals%2Fstflr60&div=55&id=&page=>

such as alternative dispute resolution (ADR) mechanisms, have also been proposed. ADR methods, such as mediation and arbitration, can provide a more efficient and cost-effective means of resolving disputes while alleviating the burden on the court system and minimizing the potential for excessive litigation.[203]

While *Donoghue v Stevenson* has been instrumental in shaping the law of negligence in Australia, its principle of duty of care has faced criticisms and limitations. Efforts to address these issues through reform proposals and alternative approaches can contribute to a more balanced and effective negligence law framework that provides adequate protection for consumers without unduly burdening businesses and public authorities.

Reflection and Significance of the Donoghue v Stevenson in Australia

The ongoing relevance and significance of *Donoghue v Stevenson* in Australia can be attributed to its enduring impact on the evolution of negligence law and consumer protection. The case established the "neighbour principle", introducing a duty of care that extends beyond contractual relationships and revolutionizing the understanding of liability in negligence cases. Its influence can be observed in the development of Australian case law, legislative reforms, and policy considerations.

Donoghue v Stevenson has shaped numerous Australian cases that have expanded and refined the concept of negligence. Landmark decisions such as *Grant v Australian Knitting Mills Ltd* and *Rogers v Whitaker* have built upon the foundation laid by *Donoghue v Stevenson*, applying the principle of duty of care to diverse contexts such as product liability and medical negligence.[204] [205]

---

203   Alexander JS Colvin, Brian Klaas, and Douglas Mahony, "Research on alternative dispute resolution procedures," (1 January 2006), online: Research on Alternative Dispute Resolution Procedures https://ecommons.cornell.edu/handle/1813/76027.

204   Chalmers and Schwartz, *supra* note 100

205   Friedmann, *supra* note 99

These cases highlight the adaptability and continuing relevance of the principles established in *Donoghue v Stevenson* within the Australian legal system.

In addition to its influence on case law, the principles established in *Donoghue v Stevenson* have been incorporated into Australian legislation, such as the *Australian Consumer Law* (ACL). The ACL enshrines the duty of care owed by manufacturers and suppliers to consumers, reflecting the case's impact on consumer protection and product safety standards. By embedding the principles of *Donoghue v Stevenson* in legislation, the case's significance is reinforced, ensuring its ongoing relevance in the legal landscape.

Moreover, the case has prompted critical discussions on the scope of the duty of care, its application to various contexts, and the need for reform. These conversations highlight the case's continuing influence on contemporary legal debates and its role in shaping future developments in negligence law.

The principles established in *Donoghue v Stevenson* have also been influential in shaping the approach to liability in other common law jurisdictions. The 'neighbour principle' has been adopted and applied in countries such as the United States, Canada, and the United Kingdom, demonstrating the case's far-reaching impact and international significance.

The ongoing relevance and significance of *Donoghue v Stevenson* in Australia are evident through its lasting impact on case law, legislation, and policy considerations. The case has played a key role in shaping the foundation of negligence law and consumer protection, prompting the evolution of legal principles and fostering critical discussions on the scope and application of the duty of care. Its influence has extended beyond Australian law and has been felt in other common law jurisdictions, demonstrating the enduring significance of this landmark case.

Chapter 10: Conclusion

Massa Mohamed Ali

From preserving justice to maintaining peace and security to promoting social and economic development, the rule of law is fundamental to society. It ensures that every individual, regardless of
their position, is subject to the same laws that are enforced fairly
and impartially. This promotes democratic values and civic participation, as everyone is treated equally under the law regardless
of their race, gender, ethnicity, or socio-economic background.
This also helps prevent the outbreak of civil unrest, as conflicts
can be resolved through legal means rather than through violence.
Not only does the rule of law protect human rights, but it also
creates predictability and stability, which creates an appropriate
environment for business growth and strengthens the economy.
Generally, courts create expectations for future actions and that
business will be conducted fairly. The legal system is one of the
most important ways society upholds the principles of the rule
of law. The legal system branches into many different areas,
including civil, family, criminal, employment, constitutional, and
administrative law.[206]

Previous chapters of this book have highlighted the independence
of the judiciary, the importance of due process, the role of legal

---

206   Government of Canada, Department of Justice. "Definitions"
(1 September 2021) online: *Government of Canada, Department of
Justice* <https://www.justice.gc.ca/eng/csj-sjc/ccs-ajc/06.html>.

aid in access to justice, the lasting influence of the famous Donoghue versus Stevenson case, and more. This chapter addresses the
need for continued efforts to preserve and strengthen the rule of
law at the individual, government, and international levels.

Role of the individual

Despite the importance of the rule of law, it is under threat
in many parts of the world. While many think that the role of
the individual when it comes to the rule of law is negligible in
comparison to the role of governments and international organizations, this perception is not entirely accurate. Individuals
have the power to influence the rule of law in their daily actions
that accumulate over time, especially when united for a specific
cause. Individuals promote and strengthen the rule of law when
they support democratic institutions, are actively involved in
the community, volunteer at several organizations, hold governments accountable, and challenge discrimination, prejudice, and
injustice. This is highlighted with more specific examples in the
following few paragraphs.

One manner in which individuals can promote the rule of law is
through their support of democratic institutions. This can be done
through voting in elections, attending town hall meetings, con-
tributing to public debates, and being a jury member. As a Canadian citizen, being a jury member is mandatory and is a good way
that individuals can be active participants in the rule of law system.[207] If an individual knows a particular subject, they can even
help the court with answers to technical questions and be called
an expert witness.[208] Another way that individuals can actively
participate in the rule of law is to attend court proceedings in the
Superior Court of Justice. Almost all court proceedings, filings,

207   Government of Canada, Department of Justice. "The role of
the public" (1 September 2021) online: *Government of Canada, Department of Justice* <https://www.justice.gc.ca/eng/csj-sjc/just/12.html#:~:-
text=Any%20adult%20Canadian%20citizen%20can,the%20laws%20
of%20their%20province.>.

208   *Ibid.*

exhibits, and audio recordings are open to the public.[209] Exceptions include sealed courtrooms with private hearings for specific cases. This can include child welfare and youth matters to protect the identity of the children and young persons. For instance, court hearings from the Children's Aid Society and proceedings involving youth criminal offenders are kept private.[210] Aside from the few exceptions, all other cases remain open for the public to attend. Attending court proceedings is beneficial for various reasons, as it allows individuals to understand how legal rules apply in practice and analyze the applications of the rule of law.

Additionally, individuals can support and get involved in organizations like the Canadian Civil Liberties Association (CCLA), which challenges unconstitutional laws and policies to advocate for civil liberties and human rights. Founded in 1964, the CCLA is known for advocating for the rights and freedoms of all persons living in Canada while addressing issues involving national security, censorship, capital punishment, and police and state accountability.[211] The CCLA describes its team as an "independent, national, nongovernmental organization, working in the courts, before legislative committees, in the classrooms, and the streets, protecting the dignity and rights of people in Canada."[212] Not only do they have a press and broadcast media presence, but they also reach over 10,000 students every year through their various workshops, seminars, and in-class sessions.[213] They continually educate citizens about their rights and freedoms, therefore promoting the strengthening and preserving of the rule of law. When

209   Ontario Courts, maintained by the Judges' Library, "Ontario Court of Justice" online: *Public and Media Access to Court Proceedings, Ontario Court of Justice* <https://www.ontariocourts.ca/ocj/covid-19/public-and-media-access-to-court-proceedings/>.

210   "Providing access to personal information under the *Child, Youth and Justice Act*" online: *Information and Privacy Commissioner of Ontario* <https://www.ipc.on.ca/wp-content/uploads/2019/11/cyf-sa-guide.pdf>.

211   CCLA, "About Us" (16 July 2021) online: *CCLA* <https://ccla.org/about-us/>.

212   *Ibid.*

213   *Ibid.*

students ranging from primary to graduate levels know how they can protect human rights and combat injustice, they can hold governments accountable for generations to come.

Recently, the CCLA has been working with the National Council of Canadian Muslims (NCCM) to challenge the government of Quebec's Bill-21 mandate in court. Bill-21 bans all religious symbols, such as hijabs, crosses, turbans, and yarmulkes in public professions.[214] This violates individuals' freedom of religion, promotes systemic discrimination, and has devastating impacts on Canada's diverse population. Ways to get involved include participating in protests opposing the bill, signing petitions, writing to the premier, education minister, and member of parliament, and raising awareness around the community and social media.[215] Laws like Bill-21 emphasize the importance of organizations like CCLA and NCCM for protecting Canadians' rights and freedoms.

These organizations become especially important during times of crisis, such as the period of the COVID-19 pandemic. In January 2021, the CCLA published a detailed report on Canadian rights during the second wave of the virus. The report addresses COVID-19's impacts on those imprisoned, homeless, indigenous, living with a disability, older adults, and more while outlining one's rights and freedoms in each case. It also details the impacts of travel restrictions and one's a constitutional right to move freely across the country.[216]

Another organization that individuals can take part in to promote and strengthen the rule of law is Innocence Canada. This is a Canadian non-profit that identifies, supports, and exonerates individ-

---

214   NCCM, "NCCM and CCLA launch legal challenge against Quebec's Bill 62" online: *NCCM* <https://www.nccm.ca/nccm-and-ccla-launch-legal-challenge-against-quebecs-bill-62/>.

215   CCLA, "Bill 21", (4 November 2022) online: *CCLA* <https://ccla.org/major-cases-and-reports/bill-21/>.

216   Government of the USA, "PEPFAR technical guidance in context of covid-19 pandemic" online: *Government of the USA* <https://www.state.gov/wp-content/uploads/2021/06/06.23.21-PEPFAR-Technical-Guidance-During-COVID-final.pdf>.

uals who have been wrongly convicted of a crime.[217] Individuals can support organizations like this by donating money, raising awareness, or providing pro bono services if qualified. Qualified individuals, including lawyers, paralegals, and law students, can also get involved with Pro Bono Students Canada (PBSC), which promotes the preservation and strengthening of the rule of law as well. PBSC's mission is to provide free legal information and services to people and communities that face several barriers to justice. In partnership with community organizations and supervising lawyers, PBSC engages around 1,500 law students every year to provide free legal support to those in need.[218] As law students are future lawyers and judges, they have a critical role in ensuring that the legal system operates following the principles of the rule of law.

The Canadian Bar Association is another excellent resource for law students in Canada, offering a range of opportunities to get involved in the legal community and develop their skills through volunteer work and pro bono initiatives. By providing legal services to those who cannot afford them, law students can help to address the inequalities and injustices that exist within the legal system and promote greater social justice.[219] Additionally, law schools should provide students with a comprehensive education of the law to ensure that future leaders and advocates of the legal profession preserve and strengthen the rule of law. This includes mandating courses about Indigenous rights, Indigenous law and Indigenous-Crown relations, for instance. As of June 2022, three law schools in Canada offer a course in Indigenous law that is mandatory for all students.[220] More law schools have mandated

217   Innocence Canada, "About Us" online: *Innocence Canada* <https://www.innocencecanada.com/about-us/>.

218   PBSC, "Who we are" online: *PBSC* <https://www.probonostudents.ca/who-we-are>.

219   The Canadian Bar Association, "CBA-FLSC Ethics Forum" (27 February 1970) online: *The Canadian Bar Association* <https://www.cba.org/Home>.

220   CBC News, "28. require all law students to take a course in Aboriginal people and the law" online: *CBC News* <https://www.cbc.ca/newsinteractives/beyond-94/require-all-law-students-to-take-a-course-

an indigenous law course for their students since then, including the University of Western Ontario and Osgoode Hall Law School.

Furthermore, individuals can advocate for access to information laws and support investigative journalism, emphasizing the need for greater transparency in government decision-making. In Canada, the Access to Information Act gives Canadian citizens, permanent residents, and those present the right to access non-personal information in federal government records.[221] This helps keep elected officials accountable and it is up to the individual to keep following the records. Similarly, investigative journalism follows specific cases to reveal all relevant facts to the public. This puts the spotlight on a wide range of issues, including corruption, human rights abuses, political scandals, and corporate wrongdoings. Individuals can stay up-to-date by attending public meetings and town halls, along with organizing peaceful protests against any injustice they see.

Role of government

Within three years, almost half of the Canadian adult population will encounter a serious legal issue.[222] Without the support of the government and a strong legal justice system, society can experience several negative consequences. Governments must address the several different barriers to justice. One way this can happen is through the funding of legal aid programs. Although access to justice is considered a fundamental right, legal representation is often unfortunately out of reach for those with limited financial

in-aboriginal-people-and-the-law#:~:text=Analysis%3A,is%20mandatory%20for%20all%20students>.

221   Branch, Legislative Services, "Consolidated federal laws of Canada, Access to Information Act" (30 March 2023) online: *Access to Information Act* <https://laws-lois.justice.gc.ca/eng/acts/a-1/page-1.html>.

222   Government of Canada, Department of Justice, "Access to justice" (1 September 2021) online: *Government of Canada, Department of Justice, Electronic Communications* <https://www.justice.gc.ca/eng/csj-sjc/access-acces/index.html>.

resources. Legal aid provides services to low-income clients who cannot afford the expenses of hiring a lawyer. The funding helps protect the rights of vulnerable populations, including children, seniors, and those living in poverty.[223] This is particularly important in family law cases, where disputes over custody, access, and support can have a significant impact on the lives of children and families. Legal aid can also assist in promoting the use of restorative justice practices in Indigenous communities, which can be more effective in resolving disputes than traditional court proceedings.[224] This promotes and strengthens the rule of law within Indigenous peoples and ensures that they are well-represented. In addition, legal aid funds legal clinics at law schools, which provide essential legal services to different populations in need.

Without legal aid, low-income individuals and marginalized communities would be left without adequate representation in court, leading to unjust outcomes in legal proceedings. Rather than being left without representation, some individuals choose to represent themselves in court. This can create several issues, as it can cause delays, inefficiencies, and potentially unjust outcomes. Legal aid can help ensure that individuals receive proper legal representation, reducing the strain on the courts and promoting a more efficient justice system.

However, due to eligibility requirements, not everyone who cannot afford a lawyer can access legal aid. And although legal aid is an important resource for those in need, there are several limitations to the services it can provide. Legal aid may provide services such as advice and representation for criminal and family law matters, but may not cover other types of legal issues. This can be problematic for people who need legal assistance for issues that are not covered by legal aid, such as immigration or civil litigation. Furthermore, legal aid certificates given to individuals must also give sufficient access to legal services. This includes

223   Legal Aid, "About lao" online: *Legal Aid Ontario* <https:// www.legalaid.on.ca/more/corporate/about-lao-landing-page/#:~:text=-Legal%20Aid%20Ontario%20(LAO)%20provides,refugee%20and%20 immigration%20law>.

224   *Ibid.*

enough access to court and a reasonable expiration date, giving lawyers the necessary time to address their client's needs. In addition to time restraints, several challenges can arise in maintaining the quality of services funded by legal aid due to the high demand for these services and the limited number of resources available by and to legal aid organizations. As a result, people who receive legal aid may not always receive the same quality of service as those who can afford to hire a lawyer, which can lead to injustice and a weakening of the rule of law. Therefore, the government must ensure that sufficient funding is provided for those unable to afford legal services. This can also include investments in legal technologies and access to justice services. Technological advancements include artificial intelligence tools for document review, legal research, and contract analysis, which can all increase the efficiency of the justice system.

Although not affiliated with the government, the Canadian Human Rights and Freedoms Centre is providing an initiative named the People's Legal Café, which ensures more equal and efficient legal access for individuals and organizations with limited financial resources. As per their website, "the Legal Café will provide simplicity for lawyers and legal assistants by managing court forms in a way that online applications like DivorceMate have simplified calculations for child support, spousal support, and special expense calculations." [225] They also mention that "through the technology of the People's Legal Café website, court form rejections will be significantly decreased which will reduce delays at the courts and create cost savings for the courts." [226] Moreover, the Legal Café will not be limited to an online application. While the application will simplify the process of completing complex court forms for the self-representing public, lawyers, and courts, the Legal Café will also exist as a storefront. It can be present in public library locations, for instance, to support self-representing individuals to file the required forms.[227] Governments could sup-

---

225   Human Rights & Freedoms Centre, "Legal café" online: *Human Rights and Freedoms Centre* <http://www.canrightsandfreedoms. ca/legal-cafeacute.html>.

226   *Ibid.*

227   *Ibid.*

port initiatives like this, along with other technological advancements in the field, to ease the burden on individuals facing legal issues.

Though technology can solve some access to justice issues, it cannot solve all of them. The Department of Justice Canada is aiming to have a people-centred approach to justice, where access to information, policies, and programs is provided to "promote peaceful and inclusive societies for sustainable development, provide access to justice for all, and build effective, accountable, and inclusive institutions at all levels." [228] This is following the main principle of the United Nation's Sustainable Development Goal 16 (SDG 16) as part of their 2030 Agenda for Sustainable Development.[229] The UN's Agenda is discussed in further detail in the *Role of international organizations* section below. Moreover, Justice Canada is investing in research, data collection, innovation, and partnerships to ensure transparency and accountability and improve access to justice.[230] The department promotes open government and open justice, both of which promote the involvement of the public in the legal system.[231] Open government initiatives include providing public access to government documents, data, and information, as well as soliciting public feedback and input on policy decisions. Open justice initiatives aim to increase public access to court proceedings, legal documents, and other information related to the justice system. By promoting open government and open justice, the Department of Justice seeks to foster public trust in the legal system and ensure that it operates in the best interests of the people it serves.

228　Government of Canada, Department of Justice, "Access to justice" (1 September 2021) online: *Government of Canada, Department of Justice, Electronic Communications* <https://www.justice.gc.ca/eng/csj-sjc/access-acces/index.html>.

229　United Nations, "The 2030 agenda for sustainable development" online: *United Nations* <https://sustainabledevelopment.un.org/content/documents/21252030%20Agenda%20for%20Sustainable%20Development%20web.pdf>.

230　*Ibid* at 141.

231　*Ibid.*

Role of international organizations

More than five billion people worldwide, making up about two-thirds of the world's population, do not have meaningful access to justice. [232] International organizations, such as the United Nations, have a critical role in promoting the rule of law and protecting human rights around the world. However, their effectiveness in achieving these goals can be limited by biases and power imbalances within the organization and in the global political system. The media coverage of Ukraine, in contrast to the Middle East, is an example of this phenomenon. In recent years, Ukraine has received significant attention from the international community. The coverage of Ukraine in the media and by international organizations has been extensive, with numerous reports, investigations, and diplomatic efforts aimed at resolving the country's political and security issues. However, the situation regarding the Middle East is different, as media coverage and international attention are often lacking in this area of the world. This imbalance creates room for injustice and misinformation. While the media should continue covering Ukraine, they should also address the injustice occurring in other, less represented countries, where unbiased enforcement of the rule of law is also needed.

Among the many Middle Eastern countries where the rule of law needs to be implemented, strengthened, and preserved, is Palestine. The United Nations has repeatedly called for Israel to comply with international law and respect the human rights of Palestinians and their property. Israel has a history of violating the human rights of Palestinians, including the right to freedom of movement, the right to education, and the right to health care.[233] Other countries in the Middle East, including Iraq, Afghanistan, and Yemen, have also experienced ongoing conflicts, resulting in instability, displacement, and human suffering. In response, the UN has implemented various peacekeeping and

232   *Ibid.*

233   Amnesty International, "Chapter 3: Israeli settlements and international law" (29 July 2021) online: *Amnesty International* <https://www.amnesty.org/en/latest/campaigns/2019/01/chapter-3-israeli-settlements-and-international-law/>.

humanitarian initiatives but this has not been sufficient. Further action is required to address the ongoing injustice, prioritize the protection of human rights, including supporting refugees, and promote sustainable peace.

The UN's 2030 Agenda for Sustainable Development aims to promote global peace and justice. The 17 Sustainable Development Goals (SDGs) of this agenda provide a comprehensive framework for sustainable development, covering a broad range of issues, including poverty, education, health, gender equality, and climate change.[234] Working closely with the UN to achieve the SDGs by 2030 is the Task Force on Justice, which was established in 2019 by a group of states and international organizations to promote peaceful, just, and inclusive societies, particularly in areas affected by conflict. Their "Justice for All" report calls for increased investments in justice systems to provide legal empowerment and accountability around the world.[235]

Most recently, several countries and organizations attempted to help the Middle East when an earthquake with a magnitude of 7.8 struck southern and central Turkey and northern and western Syria.[236] Of these organizations, the White Helmets have been recognized for their commitment to neutrality, impartiality, and humanity, which are core principles of international humanitarian law. They were originally a group of volunteers who worked to rescue people from the rubble of buildings destroyed by bombings during the Syrian Civil War.[237] They have been credited with saving thousands of lives since their founding in 2012 and operate in extremely dangerous conditions, often rushing into bombed

234   *Ibid* at 142.

235   Justice Task Force, "Task Force on justice" online: *Justice Task Force* <https://www.justice.sdg16.plus/task-force-on-justice>.

236   Center for Disaster Philanthropy, "2023 Turkey-Syria earthquake" (28 March 2023), online: *Center for Disaster Philanthropy* <https://disasterphilanthropy.org/disasters/2023-turkey-syria-earthquake/>.

237   Syria Civil Defence, "An introduction" online: *Syria Civil Defence* <https://www.syriacivildefence.org/en/who-we-are/an-introduction-to-the-white-helmets/>.

buildings to extract survivors while bombs are still falling.[238] In the case of the recent earthquake, the White Helmets rushed to rescue survivors and protect their right to life. The response of the White Helmets highlights the important role that international volunteer organizations can have in protecting human rights, particularly in areas where government resources are limited or unavailable. Despite the ongoing conflict in Syria, the White Helmets have continued to provide essential services to those in need, and their work in response to the earthquake in Turkey and Syria is yet another example of their commitment to serving their communities.

Conclusion

While there have been several advancements in the preservation and strengthening of the rule of law to date, a lot of improvement is still needed at the individual, government, and international levels. Of the numerous ways individuals can strengthen the rule of law, they can start by supporting access to justice, including advocating for legal aid programs, pro bono legal services, and the development of innovative yet efficient legal technologies. Individuals can also stay up-to-date within their community by being actively involved. This can be done through volunteering at legal organizations, attending court proceedings, holding governments accountable, signing petitions, protesting against injustice, challenging discrimination, and more. At the government level, funding for legal aid must be increased and provided regularly, as it serves those who cannot access legal services due to financial constraints. Governments must also continue to promote open government and open justice to improve the access to justice for all individuals. Lastly, international organizations have a crucial role in promoting the rule of law and protecting human rights.

---

238   *Ibid.*

They have a responsibility to do this with a consistent, impartial, and unbiased view, free of political interference and discrimination. The United Nations 2030 Agenda for Sustainable Development is a promising plan to address various ongoing conflicts, inequalities, and injustices around the world in the coming days.

Afterword

Perhaps more questions have been raised than answered. Or, perhaps the convoluted and complex nature of common law's development has left readers befuddled. In either instance, the book achieves its objective: to elucidate upon the Rule of Law.

The common law has a rich and nuanced history, and this book has taken to exploring its "rule of law" underpinnings, important cases such as *Donoghue v Stevenson*, and discussed the duty of care principle in relative detail as a case study. As demonstrated by the similarities and differences between nation-states, the common law, and with it the rule of law, has changed over time. Even something such as duty of care can have subtle distinctions as to its applicability in different countries due to differences in case law.

We encourage readers to consider what they have learned, be daring, and consider the rule of law and its implications on societal development and everyday livelihoods. Thank you for reading.

www.ingramcontent.com/pod-product-compliance
Lightning Source LLC
Chambersburg PA
CBHW021820190326
41518CB00007B/670